Supporting the Mental Health Needs of Veterans in the Metro Detroit Area

Terri Tani
Michael L. H
Laurie T. Ma
Geoffrey Gri
Cordaye Ogletree

Sponsored by the Wins for Warriors Foundation
and the Ethel and James Flinn Foundation

RAND HEALTH

For more information on this publication, visit www.rand.org/t/RR1346

Library of Congress Cataloging-in-Publication Data
is available for this publication.

ISBN: 978-0-8330-9257-1

Published by the RAND Corporation, Santa Monica, Calif.
© Copyright 2016 RAND Corporation

RAND® is a registered trademark.

Cover Images: photograph of veteran courtesy of Bill Mattocks;
sculpture photo: sj carey/Flickr

Support RAND
Make a tax-deductible charitable contribution at
www.rand.org/giving/contribute

www.rand.org

Preface

Supporting the mental health needs of veterans is a national priority. Over the past decade, there have been several studies describing the needs of the veteran population, particularly those who served in the post-9/11 era, calling for improved access to high-quality mental health services. In response, the federal government has expanded funding and services to meet increasing demand. At the same time, there has also been a proliferation of nongovernmental support to improve services for veterans in local communities. Often, in an attempt to deploy resources quickly, new programs and services are implemented without a full understanding of the specific needs of the population. This study was designed to gather information on the mental health–related needs facing veterans in the Detroit metropolitan area to identify gaps in the support landscape and inform future investments for community-level resources to fill the identified gaps.

This study was sponsored by the Wins for Warriors Foundation and the Ethel and James Flinn Foundation. The research was conducted in RAND Health, a division of the RAND Corporation. A profile of RAND Health, abstracts of its publications, and ordering information can be found at www.rand.org/health

Contents

Figures and Tables

Summary

Over the past decade, there has been a growing recognition of the challenges faced by U.S. veterans, including mental health problems such as posttraumatic stress disorder (PTSD), substance misuse, depression, and suicide. Most of the research done to understand the size and scope of the mental health issues facing this group has focused on problems at either the national level, within very specific settings—such as the Department of Veterans Affairs (VA)—or within specific local or regional units—such as National Guard units. What have often been lacking are state- or local-level assessments of veterans' mental health issues that provide context on the specific challenges facing particular veteran populations.

In an effort to inform future investments in expanding or coordinating mental health support in the metro Detroit area (Wayne, Oakland, and Macomb counties), RAND was asked to document the types of mental health issues facing veterans living in the region and identify gaps in the provision of services targeted to them. This is a particularly urgent concern in the region, which has only in the past several years begun to make significant progress recovering from a period of serious economic decline; with approximately 225,000 veterans living in the metro Detroit area—and high poverty rates among them—it is unclear whether veterans' needs are being met during this period of revitalization.

Study Methods

To assess the mental health needs and service landscape of metro Detroit area veterans, we used multiple methods that included: a review of the literature describing the veteran population, the mental health sector within the state, and the veteran support community in and around the metro Detroit area; a review of publicly available data from the VA and public information on organizations and service providers that work with veterans; stakeholder interviews focused on service providers and veteran-support government and nongovernmental organizations across the region; and focus groups and interviews with veterans aimed at gathering qualitative data on the types of mental health–related issues and challenges that veterans in the region face.

Understanding Postdeployment and Postmilitary Mental Health Problems

Risk Factors

Though not all service members will experience mental health problems, research shows that such issues are common across this population. This research has shown that exposure to combat, for example, is particularly related to PTSD and depression. Females are at increased risk for depression and males are at increased risk for substance use; however, findings are mixed with respect to PTSD and gender. PTSD is also more associated with younger age groups, individuals who are single and those who are not as satisfied in their romantic relationship. The limited number of studies that have examined race and education as risk factors for PTSD, depression, and substance misuse suggests that these may not be strong risk factors among military populations, particularly after accounting for combat experience. Finally, we looked at the evidence for military risk factors, such as service branch and rank, related to PTSD, depression, and substance misuse and found that, while studies indicate that PTSD is more prevalent in the Army and Marine Corps, and among enlisted personnel compared to officers, the failure to control for combat exposure makes the findings inconclusive.

Consequences Associated with Mental Health Problems

RAND's 2008 model of the consequences of postcombat mental health and cognitive conditions provided a useful framework to assess the consequences that veterans may face. The model highlights that consequences may be direct and short term as well as indirect and longer term, and may be affected by individual resources and vulnerabilities. We also looked more closely at the literature on the potential consequences of mental health problems, including comorbidity with other mental health problems and suicide (including substance misuse); physical health and mortality; employment and productivity; homelessness; and marriage, parenting, and child outcomes.

Treatment

Notwithstanding the serious short- and long-term consequences of mental health problems, evidence-based treatments for PTSD and depression do exist. However, not all veterans who need mental health care will seek it out, nor are all providers trained to deliver such care. Prior research suggests that a significant gap exists between mental health care needs and access. In addition, treatment of co-occurring conditions, particularly mental health problems and substance abuse, continues to present challenges due to differences in treatment philosophies, funding streams, and administrative and regulatory environments. Thus far, efforts to integrate treatment have been limited.

Challenges Facing Veterans in the Metro Detroit Area

Individual interviews and focus groups conducted with metro Detroit area veterans highlighted the major issues they faced, from their separation from the military to the present day. We note that concerns were similar across veterans of different eras and similar to those expressed by veterans in other communities.

Although questioning was not limited to mental health issues, concerns with adjustment to civilian life and mental health problems were among the predominant challenges identified. In particular, many veterans perceived that the support and regimentation of military life were lacking when they returned to civilian life. This transition to civilian life included challenges with reestablishing relationships with family and friends, accessing needed services and benefits, and finding and maintaining meaningful employment. Many of the veterans with whom we spoke noted that the speed with which a service member returns to civilian life can be problematic; while historically a "decompression" period could take weeks, service members may now transition from combat to home in as little as three days.

Many metro Detroit area veterans with whom we spoke noted that services were available to aid them during their transition; however, there was concern that awareness of and access to these services were lacking. Many indicated that they had gone years without taking advantage of available financial and medical benefits; indeed, data from the VA indicate that Michigan veterans are among the least likely in the nation to receive or take advantage of their benefits. Veterans also pointed to difficulties navigating local and federal processes to access services and claim benefits. Furthermore, logistical barriers, such as limited public transportation in the metro Detroit area, were reported to limit care seeking. Notwithstanding the aim of the VA Choice Act of 2014 to expand the network of available service providers, many veterans with whom we spoke expressed discomfort with receiving treatment from civilians, who they felt may not have sufficient familiarity with the experience of being a veteran to provide adequate care.

Beyond the above-noted challenges of transitioning to civilian life, veterans pointed to particular concerns with respect to addressing mental health problems. Among these, they noted that many service members and veterans do not recognize that they suffer from mental health problems and, for those who do, the perceptions surrounding mental health problems can keep them from accessing needed care. Even when they do access care, some veterans felt that their mental health concerns are likely to be dismissed by the VA if they had not served in a combat position. In addition, some veterans expressed concern about treatment modalities commonly used (for example, regarding overmedication). Veterans also reported concern that family members may be unprepared to support them with mental health problems.

Mental Health Support Services and Resources Available to Metro Detroit Region Veterans

Our review of organizations in the metro Detroit area that provide services and support to veterans looked at federal, state, and county government offices as well as nongovernment organizations. We found that access to specific resources may depend on the characteristics of an individual's military service and discharge status, creating a distinction between those services that are available to veterans based on meeting certain eligibility requirements, and those available to all veterans, regardless of status.

For veterans who meet conditions such as minimum active service time and discharge "under conditions other than dishonorable," we identified the following services and supports.

- *Department of Veteran Affairs:* In Michigan, the VA, which provides health care services to eligible veterans, has five VA Medical Centers, six outpatient clinics, 18 community-based outpatient clinics, and eight vet centers across the state. Within the metro Detroit area specifically, the John D. Dingell VA Medical Center is the largest provider of mental health care services for veterans, and includes a wide array of programs dedicated to mental health. In addition to the main VA Medical Center, which is located in downtown Detroit, satellite clinics and centers throughout the surrounding counties offer varied mental health care services.
- *State-based and state-funded resources:* The Michigan Veterans Affairs Agency (MVAA), which is housed within the Michigan Department of Military and Veteran Affairs, works to decrease barriers and increase access to education, employment, health care, and quality of life for eligible veterans residing in Michigan. For veterans with an honorable discharge and at least 180 days

of service during a period of war, the MVAA runs a program through the Michigan Veterans Trust Fund that pays for up to five community mental health service provider visits for a veteran who is eligible for federal benefits but not currently registered in the VA health care system.

- *County-based services and resources:* Each of the three counties comprising the metro Detroit area have county-level veteran affairs departments that facilitate access to federal and state benefits to veterans who are county residents. Wayne County Veterans Affairs focuses on financial hardship issues, while Macomb and Oakland county veteran services mainly assist veterans and their families applying for federal, state, and county benefits. For the most part, veterans with mental health–related needs are referred to local vet centers or the VA Medical Center in Detroit.
- *Nongovernmental organization services:* The many veteran service organizations in metro Detroit focus primarily on helping connect veterans to each other and sharing information about the available benefits and services that support local veterans. While none of the organizations we identified provides mental health services directly, most offer referrals to relevant service providers. Targeted programs in the region also offer support with employment and career planning, training, and housing services.

Beyond those services restricted to veterans who meet specific eligibility criteria, we identified a number of local organizations that support veterans regardless of discharge status, through mental health service provision and advocacy, as well as housing and wraparound services. Looking specifically at mental health services, we found the metro Detroit area to have a variety of individual service providers, who work through large health systems, in private clinics, or through solo practices. In recent years, several organizations have undertaken efforts to increase awareness of and access to these providers. While community mental health agencies, such as the Detroit Wayne Mental Health Authority, also provide care, their use by veterans is limited.

Despite the variety and number of organizations working to support metro Detroit area veterans, there are concerns that these entities operate independently from one another. Since 2013, MVAA's Veteran

Community Action Team has been working to promote community collaboration to deliver service and support to veterans more effectively. Other critical gaps in the service environment that were identified by stakeholders included eligibility requirements and restrictions related to the distribution and use of funding.

Recommendations for Improving Support

To sustainably and effectively meet the needs of metro Detroit area veterans, a comprehensive approach is needed to pursue the following recommendations simultaneously.

- *Raising awareness:* To strengthen support to veterans, stakeholders should work to increase awareness across diverse organizations—including community-based mental health providers—regarding the challenges faced by veterans, and also to empower veterans to take advantage of the mental health resources and services available to them.
- *Creating connections:* To better connect veterans in need with available services and to strengthen collaboration across provider communities, resources beyond word-of-mouth connections are needed. Local website directories can complement the existing MVAA website, which primarily features federal- and state-level resources. Other approaches include enhanced one-stop navigation assistance, for example, through a call center (such as the 1-800-MICH-VET) or MVAA and other websites that link veterans with peers or social workers for a full range of referral support. In addition, stronger connections between service providers can increase the efficiency of their outreach efforts, while stronger connections between veterans can support relationship building and promote an opportunity to learn from peers how they have overcome mental health challenges.
- *Filling gaps in resources:* Stakeholders pointed to a number of specific gaps in support, and noted attention could improve the provision of high-quality services to veterans. These gaps include

eligibility restrictions that prevent veterans with a less than honorable discharge status from accessing benefits and services; limitations on the use of state-provided block grants to community mental health agencies which prioritize the VA as a service provider for veterans; and limited capacity at vet centers to accommodate those interested in counseling services.

Acknowledgments

The authors wish to acknowledge the many individuals who spoke with us during this study. We are especially indebted to the veterans who participated in our focus groups and interviews for their willingness to share information and personal experiences. We also thank the many stakeholders and organizational representatives who shared information about the available resources in the community. We are grateful to our sponsors, Alisha Greenberg and Andrea Cole, for their continuous guidance and support. We also extend our thanks to Kendra Wilsher for her administrative support and work to coordinate the field data collection efforts as well as Katherine Pfrommer for her assistance in creating several maps for the report. Finally, we thank our quality assurance reviewers, Rajeev Ramchand and Katherine Kidder. Their constructive feedback helped improve the clarity and quality of this report.

CHAPTER ONE

Introduction

Over the past decade, there has been growing recognition of the challenges faced and sacrifices made by former members of the U.S. Armed Forces. During the era characterized by military operations in Afghanistan and Iraq, support for our nation's veterans reached an unprecedented level. While some Americans disagreed with the notion that America was at war, there was general support for deployed service members and their families. As media reports and other events continued to shed light on the nature of the challenges these veterans and families faced—including mental health problems, such as posttraumatic stress disorder, depression, and suicide—efforts to support this population drew increased attention across both the public and private sectors.

In response to concerns about access to mental health care for returning troops, the federal systems that support our veterans' mental health needs were expanded: Additional providers were hired, benefits were expanded, new screening, treatment, and support programs were created, and new research was commissioned. At the same time, efforts were taken at the state and local levels to create new programs to support deployed troops, veterans, and their families. Many of these efforts were supported by nongovernmental organizations and funded by private philanthropy or donations (Myer, 2013).

For the most part, these new benefits, programs, and services were aimed at meeting the needs of veterans of the post-9/11 generation. However, over the past decade, studies have also revealed increased need and demand for support among prior-era veterans as well, suggesting a more holistic and long-term view for supporting veterans is warranted (Desai et al., 2015; Hermes, Hoff, and Rosenheck, 2014).

Most of the research done to understand the size and scope of the mental health issues facing veterans has focused on either problems at the national level, within very specific settings—such as the Department of Veterans Affairs (VA)—or within specific local or regional units—such as National Guard units (Ramchand, Rudavsky, et al., 2015). While these data are helpful, they offer limited insight for state and community-based planning. As such, other studies have attempted to examine needs of a broader group of veterans residing in a specific area, such as within New York state or the western region of the United States (Schell et al., 2011).

This study was commissioned specifically to gather more detailed information about the mental health needs of veterans residing in the metropolitan Detroit area (referred to in this report as metro Detroit).[1] The purpose was to document the types of mental health issues facing the population living in the region and to identify gaps in the service landscape in order to inform future investments in expanding or coordinating mental health support in the region.

Veterans in Metropolitan Detroit: Some Context

The recent challenges faced by the metro Detroit area are well documented. Historically, the region has often been referred to as the Motor City because it is home to many American automotive giants. However, in 2009, the federal government bailed out General Motors and subsidiaries of Chrysler—two of the largest employers in the metro Detroit area—to prevent the potential collapse of the American automotive industry. As the auto industry suffered, so did Michigan. Since 2000, the number of employed residents has dropped by 400,000, close to 10 percent of the working population in the state; more than

---

[1]   For the purposes of this study, the metro Detroit area is defined as Wayne, Macomb, and Oakland counties. This metropolitan area is also referred to as Region 10 as part of the governor's prosperity initiative.

40 percent of this decline came in the metro Detroit area. Ultimately, after protracted periods of declining population and rising unemployment and poverty levels, the city of Detroit filed for bankruptcy in the summer of 2013, at which time the city owed close to $19 billion to creditors, making it the largest municipal bankruptcy case in U.S. history.

Today the metro Detroit area is undergoing rapid transformation. In December 2014, it exited bankruptcy after reaching a deal with retired city workers and creditors. Furthermore, although the metro Detroit area is still considered the auto-industry capital of the world, the metro Detroit business community now includes more service and tech-oriented businesses. Companies such as Quicken Loans, HP Enterprise Services, and Blue Cross Blue Shield of Michigan have established national and regional headquarters in the city, becoming fixtures in the downtown landscape. As of September 2015, unemployment in the metro Detroit area had fallen to 5.5 percent;[2] at 5.0 percent, unemployment in the state of Michigan fell below the national average for the first time in 15 years.

While the state, city, and its metropolitan area have all made great strides, less is known about how veterans in particular are faring during this period of revitalization. Given the high concentration of veterans in the region and the high poverty rates among veterans living in the metro Detroit area who may have been particularly affected by the loss of automotive jobs, the time is right for an in-depth analysis of the mental health and related needs of veterans.

Veteran Demographics

According to 2013 data from the U.S. Census Bureau, approximately 672,000 veterans live in the state of Michigan, making up approximately 9 percent of the state's population. Roughly one-third of the state's population resides within Region 10 and a proportionate share of veterans similarly live in the region. Figure 1.1 shows the distribution of veterans across each county in the state; aside from Wayne County,

---

[2]   It should be noted that the unemployment rate in the city of Detroit is more than twice that of the metropolitan area.

Figure 1.1
Veteran Population in Michigan by County, 2013

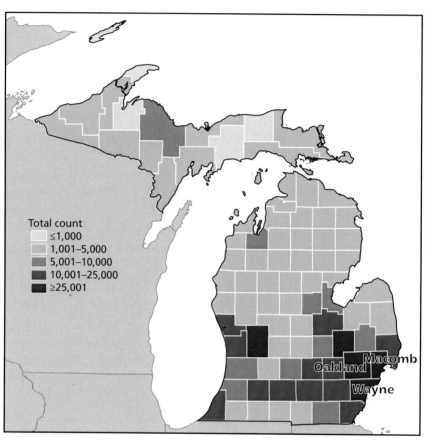

Total count
- ≤1,000
- 1,001–5,000
- 5,001–10,000
- 10,001–25,000
- ≥25,001

which includes the city of Detroit, only two other counties in the entire state have more than 25,000 veteran residents (Genesee, just northwest of Oakland county, and Kent, which is on the western side of the state). Wayne County has more veterans than any other county in Michigan, and slightly fewer than half of Region 10 veterans live in that county.

Similar to the nation as a whole, the total veteran population in Michigan and the metro Detroit area is on the decline. By 2024, the VA projects that the total veteran population in the nation will decline significantly, from 22 million in 2014 to 19 million in 2024. Within Michigan, over that same time period, it is expected to decline by 160,000. Within the metro Detroit area, the projected decline is even more pronounced: 33 percent, or from roughly 225,000 to 149,000 veterans (VA, Office of the Actuary, 2015).

Veterans Living in Poverty

Figure 1.2 shows the percentage of each county's veteran residents living below the poverty line. Within the metro Detroit area, a rela-

Figure 1.2
Percentage of Veterans Living Below the Poverty Line by County, 2013

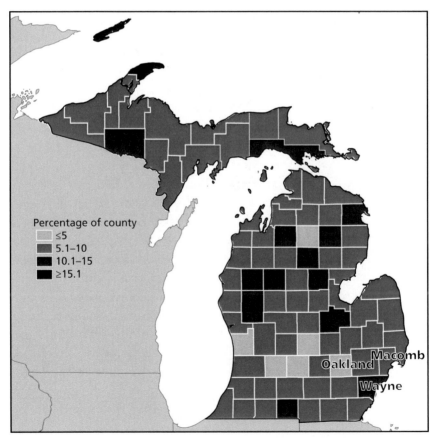

tively high proportion of Wayne County veterans are living below the poverty line; the poverty rate for veterans is approximately twice as high as the rates in Oakland and Macomb counties. Figure 1.2 also illustrates that there are other counties with poverty rates for veterans similar to that of Wayne County.

Comparison Between Veteran and Nonveteran Populations in Metro Detroit Area

Table 1.1 provides demographic information on the metro Detroit area veteran population compared with the nonveteran population in the region. These data reveal three notable differences between the two populations. First, more than 90 percent of veterans are male, compared with less than half of nonveterans. This is consistent with the fact that the U.S. military historically has been and remains predominantly male. Second, veterans residing in the region tend to be much older, even when focusing on the population that is at least 18 years of age or older. Specifically, half of the veteran population is 65 years of age or older, compared with less than 20 percent of nonveterans. Third, veterans are more likely than nonveterans to have any disability (29 percent, compared with 17 percent). These higher disability rates for veterans could reflect the relatively arduous nature of military service, but could also reflect the fact that the veteran population is older.

As Table 1.1 also shows, 77 percent of veterans in the metro Detroit area (Region 10) served during a period of war, with the largest number of veterans having served during the Vietnam Era. Post-9/11 veterans account for only about 8.5 percent of the total Region 10 veteran population. This distribution by era of service is consistent with the age distribution of all Michigan veterans (data not shown).

When compared with the profile of veterans nationally, veterans residing in the metro Detroit area look relatively similar in terms of age, gender, and percentage with a service-connected disability. Veterans in the metro Detroit region, however, are more likely to be black and have served during peacetime. Also, the proportion of post-9/11 veterans living in the metro Detroit area is much lower than the national profile of U.S. veterans.

Table 1.1
Characteristics of Veterans and Nonveterans in Metro Detroit Area

	Metro Detroit Area		Nationally	
	Percentage of Veterans	Percentage of Nonveterans	Percentage of Veterans	Percentage of Nonveterans
Age				
18–34	5.0	29.1	8.3	32.4
35–54	23.1	37.3	24.1	35.7
55–64	20.8	17.4	20.3	15.9
65–74	26.4	9.2	24.1	9.2
75 or older	24.7	7.0	23.2	6.7
Gender				
Male	93.4	44.2	92.1	44.6
Race/ethnicity				
Black	20.1	21.7	11.3	12.2
White	76.3	71.5	79.3	64.3
Any disability[a]	29.4	16.4	28.5	14.1
Era of service				
World War II	7.9	n/a	6.7	n/a
Korea	10.9	n/a	10.7	n/a
Vietnam	36.2	n/a	35.6	n/a
Gulf War (August 1990– August 2001)	13.7	n/a	18.2	n/a
Operation Enduring Freedom; Operation Iraqi Freedom; Operation New Dawn (September 2001 or later)	8.5	n/a	14.0	n/a
Peacetime	22.5	n/a	14.8	n/a

NOTE: Data are drawn from 2013 Census data and extracted from publicly available American Community Survey data.
[a] Among individuals over the age of 18 years.

VA Medical Expenditures

In fiscal year 2014, the VA served a total of 50,215 unique patients through its health care system, expending a total of $1,420,982 on medical care in the state. Given the relative concentration of veterans in metro Detroit, it is not surprising that Wayne, Oakland, and Macomb counties have the highest share of VA medical care expenditures relative to other counties in Michigan (Figure 1.3). Across the three counties, the VA spent a total of $471,361 on medical care, accounting for 33 percent of the state's total VA medical expenditures. During this

Figure 1.3
VA Medical Expenditures by County, 2014

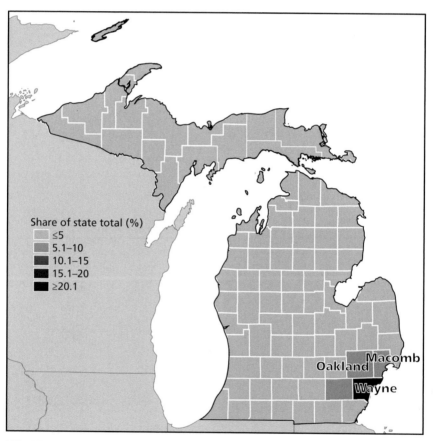

same time, a total of 44,046 unique patients were served by the VA (or 20 percent of the veteran population in the region). The John D. Dingell VA Medical Center is located in Wayne County, and accounts for more than 20 percent of the state's VA medical care costs and served 54 percent of the unique veteran patients in the region.

Previous Needs Assessment of Veterans in the Metro Detroit Area

Within Michigan, the Department of Military and Veterans Affairs serves as the primary adviser and resource to the governor on military and veteran issues. Led by the adjutant general, the department is home to the Michigan National Guard and the Michigan Veterans Affairs Agency (MVAA).[3] The MVAA was founded in 2013 to serve as the central coordinating point to connect former service members and their families with services and benefits available throughout the state, including the Michigan Veterans Trust Fund, Michigan Veterans Homes (nursing home–like facilities), and the veteran services offices in each county.[4]

In 2013, MVAA implemented the Michigan Veterans Community Action Teams (MIVCAT) project. This collaborative community model was created by the Altarum Institute and piloted in two of Michigan's ten Prosperity Regions.[5] One of these pilots was implemented in the metro Detroit area, which includes Macomb, Oakland, and Wayne counties. Concurrent with the launch of these pilots, Altarum conducted a community needs assessment on behalf of MVAA.

Released in September 2014, the Veterans Community Action Teams (VCAT) Community Assessment synthesized findings from interviews with key regional leaders, focus groups and a survey with veterans, and a survey of service providers (Altarum Institute, 2014). The VCAT Community Assessment for Region 10 focused on only

---

[3] MVAA began operations on March 20, 2013 (State of Michigan, 2013).

[4] More information on these offices, as well as the resources they offer, is in Chapter Four.

[5] As part of the Michigan Regional Prosperity Initiative, the governor designated ten "prosperity regions" across the state.

Wayne County because this was the only county for which there were lists of veterans to contact. From the survey of Wayne County veterans (405 veterans participated through convenience-based methods), Altarum identified a number of needs with respect to improving knowledge of services and benefits, ease of access to benefits and services, and satisfaction with and utilization of resources. The assessment focused on the broad areas of education, employment, and health care. In Altarum's report, mental health care was accessed by 30 percent of respondents, the majority (85 percent) of whom sought services directly from the VA. Among Wayne County veterans using mental health care services, 58 percent also indicated they were very or somewhat satisfied with the services.

While these insights into Wayne County veterans accessing mental health care are important, issues affecting veterans residing in other counties are unknown. At the same time, there is little specific information to guide the efforts of nongovernmental organizations that also offer mental health support to veterans residing in the metro Detroit area. Thus, the current study was intentionally designed to focus on issues specific to improving mental health services for veterans residing in Macomb, Oakland, or Wayne counties, regardless of whether they are currently accessing such services.

Methods

To inform our analysis, we relied upon multiple methods of information collection. All procedures were reviewed and approved by the RAND Human Subject Protections Committee and are described here.

Review of Public Information and Data. We reviewed the published scientific and gray literature that described the veteran population, the mental health service sector broadly and within Michigan, and the veteran support community in and around the metro Detroit area. We drew heavily upon existing and publicly available data from the VA about the size and characteristics of the veteran population residing in the region. To identify organizations and service providers that work with veterans, we searched the Internet and talked with local officials who work with the MVAA, as well as the directors of veterans affairs in each of the three counties: Macomb, Oakland, and Wayne.

The metro Detroit area coordinator for Give An Hour (GaH) also provided us with an informal directory of support organizations that had been collated for its own referral purposes.[6] We then gathered information about these organizations and service providers from publicly available sources and supplemented that information with interviews with representatives and stakeholders from within those organizations.

Stakeholder Interviews. To gather additional information about the nature of services and resources available to address the mental health issues facing veterans in the metro Detroit area, we conducted a series of one-on-one interviews with representatives from service-providing or veteran-support organizations across the region (referred to as "stakeholders"). We reached out to stakeholders from government (such as state and county veteran affairs personnel, community mental health services) as well as nongovernmental organizations (nonprofit entities delivering services or supports to veterans, such as veteran service organizations). We conducted a total of 16 interviews with stakeholders (three additional stakeholders were invited to participate but were nonresponsive after several attempts to schedule a discussion).

Regional stakeholders were asked to provide a brief overview and history of their organization's mission, to identify their target audience (including whether veterans were eligible for services/support), the types of operational challenges they faced in delivering services to veterans, and whether they were engaged in any regional partnerships with other veteran service organizations. We also asked these stakeholders to comment on their experience with respect to the types of mental health challenges they observed in the veteran community, about other types of mental health or social support services that may be available, and for any recommendations that could help improve the delivery of services to veterans in the region. Notes from these interviews, along with the publicly available information, were used to summarize the types of services and resources available (see Chapter Four).

---

[6] GaH is a national nonprofit organization made up of licensed or certified mental health professionals who have agreed to donate up to one hour per week to support mental health issues among veterans and their loved ones. In 2013, GaH was awarded a grant from the Wins for Warriors Foundation to expand its network of providers in the region; to do this, GaH hired a regional coordinator.

Veteran Focus Groups and Interviews. We also conducted a series of focus groups and interviews with veterans residing in the region. The purpose of these groups was not to generate representative data on the extent of the need, but to gather qualitative data on the types of mental health–related issues and challenges that veterans in the region face. For the purposes of this study, a veteran was considered anyone who had formerly served in the U.S. Armed Forces, including former members of the Active and Reserve Component (which includes National Guard).

To recruit participants for these focus groups and interviews, we asked local veteran support organizations to disseminate information about the study through their mailing lists and social media outlets. Flyers were distributed by the MVAA, as well as at meetings of the local VCAT. These flyers invited veterans residing in the metro Detroit area to join a discussion of the challenges, issues, and opportunities facing veterans and service members. The flyers gave the locations and dates of these discussions and told participants that food and beverages would be provided and that participants would receive a $25 token of appreciation. VCAT members were also asked to share information about the study opportunity through their email distribution lists and social media platforms (Facebook and Twitter). RAND provided sample language for the email and social media posts based upon the flyer.[7] Interested participants were asked to visit a landing page on the RAND website to learn more about the study and, if interested in participating, to fill out a brief online screener to register for one of the

---

[7]   A sample Facebook post read:

> Detroit Area Veterans and Reserve/Guard members: The RAND Corporation is conducting a study of the issues, challenges, and opportunities facing those of us residing in the metropolitan area. Attend one of their May 2015 sessions and receive $25 for your time. Food will also be provided. For more information, please visit www.rand.org/detroitveterans.

Sample Tweets read:

> Are you a veteran residing in Wayne, Macomb, or Oakland County? We want to hear about your experiences. To learn more, please visit www.rand.org/detroitveterans OR Motor City Veterans! We want to hear about your experiences living in Metro Detroit. To learn more, please visit www.rand.org/detroitveterans.

sessions. A toll-free number was also provided for individuals to contact RAND staff with questions. For individuals without web access, the RAND team registered them via phone. Any individual that had previously served in the U.S. Armed Forces was eligible to participate, regardless of the timing or nature of his or her military separation.

Focus groups were organized to occur over the course of one week, with groups held in each of the three counties. Women were able to register for a female-only group if they were interested, and separate groups were offered for post-9/11 and pre-9/11 veterans. Members of the National Guard and Reserve were also encouraged and invited to attend. A total of 34 veterans signed up either through the online platform or by telephone and registered for one of the scheduled groups; however, six canceled participation in the week before the sessions due to scheduling conflicts. For veterans who were unable to make one of the scheduled events, by either notifying us in advance or calling after they missed an in-person event, we conducted individual phone interviews. A total of 24 veterans participated in either a focus group or interview. Table 1.2 displays the characteristics of the participating veterans.

The veteran focus group and interviews followed a similar protocol: After reviewing the consent procedures and setting some ground rules for the discussion, participants were asked to describe the kinds of issues and challenges that veterans and their families face leaving the military and/or coming home from a deployment; to discuss and identify the types of services that are available in the area to help address any mental health challenges that veterans face; to comment on access to and quality of these types of services; and to describe any specific barriers and challenges that veterans face in getting mental health care. We also asked all participants to provide ideas and/or suggestions for improving mental health services and programs for veterans. Focus groups were audio-recorded and transcribed, and supplemented by our team's notes. Transcripts and notes were reviewed by the study team to identify themes and quotes representing the issues raised by participants.

Table 1.2
Characteristics of Veterans Participating in Focus Groups

Characteristic	N=24	%
Gender		
Male	19	70
Service branch		
Army	16	67
Navy	3	13
Air Force	4	17
Marine Corps	1	4
Coast Guard	1	4
Prior combat experience	11	46
Era of service		
Post–9/11	5	21
Gulf War	8	33
Vietnam	10	42
Other	4	17
Employment status		
Student	1	4
Unemployed	6	25
Employed	6	25
Retired	8	33
Prior use of mental health services	10	42

Organization of Report

The remainder of this report is organized into four sections. Findings from our literature review and interviews with stakeholders, as well as the focus groups and interviews with veterans, informed the analyses. Where relevant, we use quotes from our interviews to illustrate a particular issue throughout the report. In Chapter Two, we summarize the existing literature with respect to what is known about the risk factors for and consequences associated with postdeployment mental health issues among former service personnel and veterans to provide a broader context for understanding the issues facing veterans in the metro Detroit region. In Chapter Three, we expand upon many of the related challenges that veterans face that may stem from mental health challenges based upon our discussions and focus groups with veterans. In Chapter Four, we describe the types of resources, programs, and services available, and stakeholder perceptions of gaps throughout the metro Detroit region to address mental health concerns among veterans in the community, drawing upon the review of publicly available information as well as interviews with stakeholders in the region. And, finally, in Chapter Five, we identify gaps and make a series of recommendations for improving access to mental health services for veterans in the metro Detroit area.

CHAPTER TWO

Understanding Postdeployment and Postmilitary Mental Health Problems

Researchers have been studying the impact of deployment and combat exposure on mental health for decades, though the literature has expanded considerably in recent years. Since September 11, 2001, the United States has deployed more than 2.7 million men and women to support combat operations in Afghanistan and Iraq, with many individuals deploying multiple times (Ramchand, Rudavsky, et al., 2015). While not all individuals were exposed directly to combat, the majority of service members experienced lengthy periods of time away from home, and experienced the stress of supporting military operations or caring for those wounded or killed in action.

Experiencing such stress, trauma, and uncertainty has the potential to lead to a number of mental health problems, including diagnosable conditions (such as posttraumatic stress disorder [PTSD] or depression), or risky behaviors, such as substance misuse. Collectively, we refer to these issues as mental health problems.[1] Though not all service members will experience mental health problems, estimates suggest that such problems are not uncommon. Estimates vary widely, driven in part by study methods and criteria used to identify PTSD, depression, and substance misuse. In fact, "most existing studies define cases

---

[1] When used in this paper, the phrase *mental health concerns* refers to any concerns expressed around mental health issues regardless of a value attribution (good or bad), whereas the term *mental health problem* refers specifically to those concerns that may be perceived as problematic. The term *mental health condition* is used to refer to issues that have risen to the level of a diagnosable mental health illness, such as PTSD and depression.

of PTSD and depression using criteria that have not been validated, that are not commonly used in population-based studies of civilians, and that are likely to exclude a significant number of service members who have these conditions" (Tanielian and Jaycox, 2008, p. 48; Ramchand, Schell, et al., 2010). Differences in the characteristics of the study population (e.g., the proportion exposed to combat or currently seeking treatment) may also affect estimates. Among nontreatment-seeking samples, the reported prevalence of PTSD has ranged from 0 to 48 percent, the prevalence of depression from 4 to 45 percent, and the prevalence of substance misuse from 4 to 66 percent (Ramchand, Rudavsky, et al., 2015). Among treatment-seeking samples, the reported prevalence of PTSD has ranged from 2 to 68 percent, the prevalence of depression from 1 to 60 percent, and substance misuse from 3 to 60 percent (Ramchand, Rudavsky, et al., 2015; Tanielian and Jaycox, 2008). Readers interested in a more detailed review of these estimates are directed to two comprehensive reviews of the literature, conducted by RAND (Ramchand, Rudavsky, et al., 2015; Ramchand, Schell, et al., 2010). No studies have examined the prevalence of PTSD, depression, or substance misuse among veterans in Wayne, Oakland, and Macomb counties specifically.

Risk Factors

Gaining a better understanding of which service members may be more likely to develop mental health problems has the potential to inform the development or strategic placement of programs and supports before, during, and after deployment. As a result, numerous studies have sought to identify risk factors for PTSD, depression, and substance misuse in veteran populations. Risk factors under study have included both demographic characteristics (e.g., age, sex, marital status) and military characteristics (e.g., component, rank, unit morale and cohesion, deployment, injured/wounded).

Perhaps one of the better-established risk factors among veterans and service members is combat exposure, particularly for PTSD and depression (Ramchand, Rudavsky, et al., 2015; Tanielian and

Jaycox, 2008). It is important, however, to keep in mind that combat exposure is not necessarily random; some groups of individuals (i.e., infantrymen, special operations forces, enlisted) may be more likely to experience it. At the same time, however, the use of roadside improvised explosive devices in Iraq and Afghanistan placed combat support troops at significant risk, as well. As a result, some of the demographic and military-related risk factors for mental health problems may be explained, at least partially, by the fact that these groups (e.g., enlisted service personnel in combat and combat support units) are more likely to have combat exposure. While many studies control for actual combat exposure, others do not.

We review some of the more established risk factors for PTSD, depression, and substance misuse, drawing largely from the literature of those who served during the Iraq and Afghanistan eras.

Demographics

Gender and age are the two demographic characteristics most often studied in relation to risk for mental health problems. While findings consistently suggest that females are at increased risk for depression and males are at increased risk for substance use, findings are mixed with respect to PTSD; some studies show men are at higher risk, and others show women are (Ramchand, Rudavsky, et al., 2015). With respect to age, study findings suggest that younger age groups are more likely to experience symptoms or diagnosis of PTSD, though this finding is not universal. Similarly, there is a higher risk in general for PTSD and PTSD symptoms for individuals who are not in a relationship or who are not as satisfied in their relationship. Fewer studies have examined race and education as risk factors for PTSD, depression, and substance misuse—and findings have been mixed, suggesting that these may not be strong risk factors for mental health problems among military populations, particularly after accounting for combat experience (Ramchand, Rudavsky, et al., 2015).

Military Characteristics

Several studies have examined potential military risk factors (e.g., service branch, rank) for PTSD, depression, and substance misuse.

Despite a number of studies that found PTSD is more prevalent in the Army and the Marine Corps, and that PTSD is more prevalent among enlisted personnel relative to officers and inversely related to rank, none of these studies controlled for combat exposure. Given that enlisted men and women, and those in the Army and Marine Corps may be more likely to experience combat, it is not clear whether there is something specific about the branch of service or rank that places individuals at higher risk for PTSD, or whether this association is explained merely by combat exposure. While this is an important distinction from an etiologic perspective, this distinction is less important from a program or intervention perspective and may be useful for targeting of resources.

Consequences Associated with Mental Health Problems

In 2008, RAND published *Invisible Wounds of War* (Tanelian and Jaycox, 2008), a report on psychological and cognitive injuries, their consequences, and services to assist recovery. As part of that effort, RAND developed a model of the consequences of postcombat mental health and cognitive conditions, reproduced here, as it provides a helpful framework within which to think about the consequences of mental health problems that veterans may face. This model drew from two primary existing theories and perspectives on the consequences of mental health and cognitive conditions: The first is the stress-diathesis model (Zubin and Spring, 1977), which suggests that the presence of a diathesis, or vulnerability, is not enough to bring about a diagnosable mental condition on its own, but problems occur when such individuals are confronted by stress. The second perspective is the Life-Span Developmental Perspective, which seeks to inform our understanding of how mental disorders may give rise to future problems. The resulting model highlights that impairments resulting from mental health and cognitive conditions, such as traumatic brain injury (TBI), may have direct, short-term consequences, as well as indirect and longer-term consequences across the life span. The model also highlights the potential roles that individual resources (that may buffer) or vulnerabilities

Figure 2.1
A Model of Postdeployment Mental Health Consequences

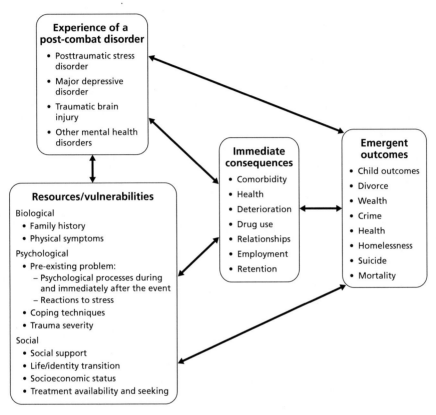

RAND RR1346-2.1

(that may exacerbate) have on these outcomes over time. Implicit in this model is the notion that the severity of symptoms can range from mild to severe, even among individuals with a similar diagnosis.

Here we briefly summarize some of the potential consequences of mental health problems, touching briefly on other mental health problems and suicide (including substance misuse); physical health and mortality; employment and productivity; homelessness; and marriage, parenting, and child outcomes. In the next section, we discuss these issues in more detail as they relate to the experiences of metro Detroit area veterans specifically.

Other Mental Health Problems

Among individuals with mental health problems, it is not uncommon to have co-occurring disorders; in other words, to have multiple mental health problems at the same time. This can be particularly challenging for individuals to navigate, as those who experience more than one mental health problem at any given time will often have negative outcomes that are more severe, more complex, or more difficult to treat than if they had only one mental health problem, and experience more disability in social and occupational functioning over time.

Though the challenges measuring the prevalence of mental health problems described earlier in this chapter applies to studies of comorbidity as well, research in the general population suggests that about 88 percent of men and 79 percent of women with PTSD also experience one other mental disorder in their lifetime (Kessler, Sonnega, et al., 1995). Among those with PTSD, the most common comorbidities are with depression, substance abuse, and other anxiety disorders. In one study of recently returned service members and veterans, approximately two-thirds of those with PTSD had probable major depression (Tanielian and Jaycox, 2008). Among those in the general population with depression in the past year, about 45 percent experienced a second diagnosis (Kessler, Chiu, et al., 2005), most commonly personality disorders (38 percent), anxiety disorders (36 percent), nicotine dependence (26 percent), and alcohol dependence (14 percent) (Hasin et al., 2005).

There is also a long-standing concern about suicide among military personnel. From 2005 to 2010, the military experienced a doubling of its suicide rate (Ramchand, Acosta, et al., 2011) and in 2012 (the year for which the most recent published rates are available) the rate remained at 23 per 100,000 (Smolenski et al., 2013), nearly double the civilian rate of 12.6 deaths per 100,000 (American Foundation for Suicide Prevention, 2013). Though markedly higher than the civilian rate, the difference is largely attenuated, though still elevated, after adjustment for demographic factors, such as age, gender, and race (Smolenski et al., 2013; Ramchand, Acosta, et al., 2011). Data on suicides among veterans are more difficult to obtain, but recent estimates from 23 states also suggest an increase in the suicide rate among veterans: In 2010, the rate was 35.9 per 100,000 lives at risk, a rate triple that of nonveterans in the same states (Hoffmire, Kemp, and Bossarte, 2015). There is a large body of evidence to suggest that mental health problems, particularly depression and TBI, increase the risk for suicide (Mann et al., 2005).

Substance use disorders (SUDs) also commonly co-occur with other mental disorders. Among the civilian population, about half of those diagnosed with substance abuse also have a mental disorder, and about 15–40 percent of people with a mental disorder are diagnosed with substance abuse (Kessler, Nelson, et al., 1996; Regier et al., 1990). While several studies have attempted to discern the temporal relationship between mental disorders and alcohol and drug misuse, the results have been mixed (Karney et al., 2008). In most cases, however, it appears that substance use often results from PTSD and often precedes depression (Kessler, Sonnega, et al., 1995).

Physical Health and Mortality

There are strong relationships between physical health and mental well-being. In some cases, mental health problems, such as trauma and PTSD, can lead to poor physical health through altered biological functions (e.g., decreased immune function) or by influencing individual health risk behaviors (e.g., smoking, poor diet) (Schnurr and Green, 2004). In other cases, concerns around physical health or chronic pain result in mental health problems or disorders (Demyttenaere et al., 2007).

Studies suggest that individuals with mental disorders, particularly depression and TBI, have higher rates of mortality, arising primarily from two causes: unnatural causes (e.g., homicide, suicide, and unintentional injuries) and cardiovascular disease (Wulsin, Vaillant, and Wells, 1999; Boscarino 2006a, Boscarino, 2006b). In fact, cardiovascular disease is one of the more commonly studied morbidities among individuals with mental disorders. One study found that individuals with depression were almost twice as likely to develop coronary heart disease compared with individuals without depression (Rugulies, 2002); individuals with PTSD are also at increased risk for coronary heart disease and heart attacks (Bankier and Littman, 2002; Boscarino and Chang, 1999; Solter et al., 2002). Aside from cardiovascular health, evidence suggests that those with a diagnosis of PTSD, depression, or TBI are more likely to report having a wide range of physical symptoms (e.g., pain in limbs, headache, dizziness, nausea) (Hoge et al., 2007). It is not surprising, therefore, that individuals with PTSD also report lower quality of life and well-being compared with those without PTSD (Magruder et al., 2004; Schnurr, Hayes, et al., 2006; Wells et al., 1989; Zatzick et al., 1997).

Employment and Productivity

Studies of the effect of PTSD on current employment status indicate that veterans with PTSD are less likely to be currently employed than veterans without the disorder (McCarren et al., 1995; Savoca and Rosenheck, 2000; Smith, Schnurr, and Rosenheck, 2005; Zatzick et al., 1997). It also has been demonstrated that as the severity of PTSD symptoms increased, the likelihood of both full-time and part-time work decreased (Smith, Schnurr, and Rosenheck, 2005). Similar studies have been conducted for depression, documenting an inverse association between depression and the probability of current employment, further supporting the notion that mental disorders can have negative consequences for employment (Savoca and Rosenheck, 2000; Ettner, Frank, and Kessler, 1997). Even when employed, having mental health conditions can affect absenteeism, or the number of lost workdays, and presenteeism, or lost productivity at work. Though this body of literature is smaller, some studies suggest that workers with depression missed an average of one hour per week due to absenteeism vs. 0.4 hours per week for those without depression (Greenberg et al., 2003; Kessler, Borges, and Walters, 1999). There is also evidence linking mental disorders with decreased wages—veterans suffering from PTSD have hourly wages that are 16 percent lower than veterans who do not, and hourly wages for those with depression were 45 percent lower than for veterans who do not (Savoca and Rosenheck, 2000).

Homelessness

Mental health problems and substance use have been described as a primary risk factor for veteran homelessness, more so than any other military factor, including combat exposure (Rosenheck et al., 1996; Roth, 1992). While several studies have examined the prevalence of mental disorders among homeless populations, it is actually not clear whether mental conditions such as depression and anxiety cause homelessness or whether being homeless increases the risk of developing such mental health problems (Gonzalez et al., 2001; Susser, Lin, and Conover, 1991). Evidence seems to point to mental health concerns being a risk factor for homelessness, however, as some studies have been able to determine the temporal relation between the two—finding, for example, that 75 percent of homeless individuals with PTSD developed the diagnosis prior to becoming homeless (North and Smith, 1992; Backer and Howard, 2007).

Homeless veterans with mental disorders are a particularly vulnerable group, as they have worse physical health and self-reported health; difficulty with subsistence needs, such as finding shelter, food and clothing; victimization; and a lower quality of life (Sullivan et al., 2000).

Marriage, Parenting, and Child Outcomes

Although mental disorders are experienced first and foremost by the service member or veteran, it is not surprising that mental health problems have a ripple effect that can affect the entire family. The cognitive and emotional deficits associated with PTSD, depression, and TBI inhibit activities crucial for maintaining intimacy in a relationship. Individuals must be capable of experiencing and expressing emotion, understanding, and providing for each other's needs, and acting in a manner consistent with that understanding (Carroll et al., 1985; Karney et al., 2008). Many mental disorders can interfere with these behaviors. It is not surprising, therefore, that major depression and depressive symptoms are strongly linked to lower levels of marital satisfaction, higher rates of marital distress, and higher rates of divorce (Jordan et al., 1992; Kessler, Walters, et al., 1998; Kulka et al., 1990; MacDonald et al., 1999; Riggs et al., 1998). Much of the literature has focused on the direct effects of mental disorders on the service member or veteran, but PTSD, depression, and TBI also have the potential to create a substantial caregiving burden on the spouse (Ramchand,

Tanielian, et al., 2014). In a similar light, challenges related to the emotional detachment caused by mental disorders can have a negative impact on parenting and child outcomes. To the extent that service members' mental disorders negatively affect their intimate relationships and parenting practices, these disorders are likely to have indirect, but long-term consequences for their children. Studies suggest that children of veterans with PTSD are more likely to experience academic problems and psychiatric treatment for their own mental health problems (Davidson, Smith, and Kudler, 1989). Children of depressed parents are at greater risk for behavioral problems, psychiatric diagnosis, and academic disruptions (Beardslee, Bemporad, et al., 1983; Beardslee, Versage, and Gladstone, 1998; Cummings and Davies, 1999).

Treatment

Despite the prevalence of mental health problems and increased risk for a range of short- and long-term outcomes, it is important to note that a number of evidence-based treatments for treating PTSD and major depression are available (Burnam et al., 2008). For PTSD, this includes therapies such as prolonged exposure therapy, trauma-focused cognitive behavioral therapy (CBT), cognitive processing therapy, and eye movement desensitization and reprocessing (EMDR). For depression, evidenced-based therapies include CBT and pharmacotherapy. These therapies typically are delivered to an individual patient by an individual provider, though other delivery modes include group therapy, marital therapy, and inpatient treatment.

Despite the availability of these treatments, not all veterans with mental health problems will seek mental health care, nor are all mental health providers trained in delivering treatment. In fact, prior research suggests a significant gap in access to care among veterans with mental health problems (Sharp et al., 2015; Tanielian and Jaycox, 2008; Zinzow et al., 2013) as well as a gap in the availability of providers equipped to deliver culturally competent evidenced-based care (Brown et al., 2015; Tanielian, Farris, et al., 2014).

Another challenge relates to how best to treat co-occurring conditions, particularly mental health and substance abuse. Historically, differences in treatment philosophies and training between substance abuse and mental health professionals, differences in funding streams for each system, and differences in state-level administrative structures and regulatory environments governing the two systems have made it difficult for individuals to obtain necessary care that will treat multiple conditions (Burnam and Watkins, 2006; Kavanagh et al., 2000; Mueser, 2003; Watkins et al., 2005). Those who did access treatment sought it either sequentially (treatment for one disorder and then the other) or in parallel (treatment for both at the same time), though the challenges noted above meant that the treatments received were not well integrated (Burnam and Watkins, 2006). More recently, there has been movement toward integrating treatment services at the client level, with multidisciplinary teams and a single treatment plan, called integrated dual disorders treatment (IDDT) (Center for Mental Health Services, 2003). While these are promising, there also may be other evidence-based practices for treating individuals with co-occurring disorders. It is unclear to what extent these practices are systematically implemented in settings that treat veterans with co-occurring disorders.

Conclusion

This chapter provides an important foundation for understanding postdeployment and postmilitary mental health problems, as well as their potential short- and long-term outcomes. Though such information is not specific to mental health problems among veterans in the metro Detroit area, there is little evidence to suggest that the risks for and consequences of mental health problems would differ. In the following chapter, we provide additional insight on these issues raised by veterans residing in the metro Detroit area and discuss the availability of mental health support services and resources to address these gaps and needs in Chapter Four.

CHAPTER THREE

Issues and Challenges of the Veteran Population Residing in the Metro Detroit Area

We asked veterans living in the metro Detroit area to describe the major issues and challenges they face. We intentionally did not limit this initial question to challenges related to mental health, in order to provide veterans the opportunity to discuss their primary concerns, although most were related to adjustment and mental health problems or their consequences. In individual interviews and focus groups, Detroit area veterans described the major issues they faced upon their initial separation from the military up through the present day in learning about and navigating services and benefits.

Though the nature of military service and the transition processes and programs have changed substantially over time, veterans of different eras of service expressed fairly similar concerns. Furthermore, the issues and challenges discussed by the veterans with whom we spoke are similar to those expressed by service members and veterans from other communities. Below, we briefly summarize the major issues and challenges reported by these veterans.

Adjusting to Civilian Life

The adjustment back to civilian life after completing military service is itself often a stressor for new veterans. While in the military, training and acculturation are intended to raise physical and mental readiness for their duties, which could include deployment and combat or combat support. This immersion in the military culture necessarily requires some separation from civilian society, interrupting regular contact with family, friends, and popular culture. Even when active-duty service members are not deployed, they live on or near military installations, which are intended to support both service members and their families. Consequently, they are provided health care and have access to child, youth, and school services; soldier and family programs; and community recreation opportunities. They are also provided housing, either on the installation or through an allowance to subsidize living in the community. These benefits are not commonly provided by private-sector employers, but are provided to service members and their families, in part, to relieve the stresses of civilian life and to allow service members to focus on their mission. Military service is also a highly regimented environment; service members are expected to follow orders, perform specific duties, and adhere to a unique structure and discipline uncommon in the private sector.

Deployments—and, for reservists, mobilizations—necessitate a physical separation from friends and family, and the experiences associated with being in or supporting combat are directly felt by the service member and not their loved ones. However, military life creates some separation even in peacetime environments. Service members are expected to drill and train with their units and are placed in an environment intended to foster cohesion with their fellow service members, their "teammates."

Returning to civilian life removes the service member from this regimented environment and can often be a challenge. As one stakeholder put it, "transition is not geographic, it's psychological. It is moving from a highly structured military culture to a much less structured civilian culture, which for many veterans can cause frustration." Many veterans recalled that loss of this structure, and the camaraderie of fellow service members, was very stressful as they began to learn a "new normal."

For many veterans, this transition requires that they reconnect with loved ones, find new employment, and connect to needed services for themselves and their families. During this period, veterans are also expected to re-acclimate themselves to civilian society. This can be challenging. One Gulf War veteran likened it to "taking somebody from another country whose culture is different than yours, and then try to have them acclimate to a totally different culture. It takes time." Other veterans with whom we spoke also echoed this general sense of lack of belonging; one individual said, "The loneliest day I ever had was the day I got out of the service." These examples point to a transition experience for which veterans did not feel adequately prepared.

A possible explanation for this challenging transition, something we heard about from many veterans, is the feeling of an *abrupt* end of service and *immediate* return to civilian life. Many veterans noted that they considered the absence of any sort of decompression period as a driver of instability, something that is exacerbated for recently deployed service members. Active duty personnel operating in combat zones can be home in America, separated from service, and expected to function as a civilian within days. One veteran pointed to the disjunctive experience of a fast transition for combat veterans: "They come home and they go from a hardcore military combat, bullets flying, bombs blowing up all over the place, and all of a sudden they're home and there's nothing going on." The service members with whom we spoke perceived that, in the past, service members had longer periods of physical transition from the combat zones. As one Vietnam Era veteran mentioned, "There needs to be a decompression period. After World War II, guys in the Asian Pacific had a decompression period for six weeks. Now they are in the battlefield, then back home in under three days."

Exacerbating these pressures is the fact that many veterans do not have civilian employment lined up before they separate from service, and often do not begin to search for jobs until after they transition. As one post-9/11 Army veteran noted about his fellow soldiers, "What they think is happening to them and what's going to happen to them is two different things. . . . They're used to a steady paycheck . . . and [think] they'll land a job as soon as they get out . . . and that was not the case." He elaborated that, even for more-senior soldiers, "unless they had a definite plan . . . meaning they had a follow-on job ready as they got out . . . they suffered as well."

The lack of full- or even part-time employment affects other aspects of a transition back to civilian life, since a steady paycheck also provides other opportunities. For example, this same veteran noted that many soldiers "had no place to stay, meaning that they had to go back [to living] with their parents and, as an adult, that's hard to do when you're living on your own and then having to turn around and go back."

Moreover, many veterans identified challenges related to re-establishing and maintaining family relationships. One veteran stated, "Your stress is elevated because you find out that your family is wanting you to be one way, and that's the way that you were prior." But for some veterans the events of war and the mental health challenges arising from those experiences alter their disposition and personality. This can be hard on family members: "They're not prepared for the issues that you have because there is no training for them . . . there's no education for them to understand." Without training, families may not be prepared to address the psychological issues veterans carry back with them from war or provide the proper support these veterans need as they work through such issues.

Some veterans with whom we spoke emphasized that these psychological challenges are not limited to service members in traditional combat occupations. During deployments to combat zones, many service members are directly exposed to combat, even if they are not on the front lines. As one post-9/11 veteran characterized it, "Just because your invoice says you do this [job], that doesn't mean that's what you do all day." He then recounted his observation of an Army sergeant deployed to Iraq as a clerk, noting "he just wasn't up there typing up s**t and making allotments of whatever else that he had to do. . . . They put him out there . . . recovering bodies."

Generally, most Detroit area veterans with whom we spoke separated from the military at least five years ago and reported feeling ill-equipped to transition from military to civilian life. Whether this was due to military-civilian culture shock, mental health issues resulting from service, lack of support, or the pressure to quickly contribute or wholly provide for the financial security of a household, transition-related frustrations often seemed to compound existing issues, resulting in additional (or more serious) problems, such as depression, divorce, and homelessness. One veteran implied that these problems are unavoidable: "The first thing that happened to me, of course, is I got divorced. That's just one of the symptoms." Another veteran reflected on the pressures meeting him in civilian life and feeling without support: "I couldn't find a job. I had a wife to support and it was tough on me . . . I started drinking and doing things, having problems with that. And I had nobody, basically, to talk to." Veterans with whom we spoke generally viewed transitioning as a critical period where those leaving the service needed support and guidance to succeed. Veterans noted that a large part of receiving that support is being able to, and knowing how to, access it in one's local community, to prevent the development of more serious mental health problems over time.

Accessing Benefits and Services

The majority of metro Detroit area veterans we interviewed had been separated from service for many years. The disappointment they expressed about their personal transition process was coupled with comments that the federal government generally, and the Department of Defense specifically, should have done more to help them. These metro Detroit area veterans said services were available during their periods of transition but that both awareness of and access to them were lacking. However, many also noted the existence of veteran service organizations to help veterans apply for federal or state benefits and services.

Many of the veterans we interviewed went years, even decades, without utilizing financial and medical benefits for which they were eligible from the VA. In fact, Michigan veterans are among the least likely in the nation to receive or take advantage of their VA benefits. According to data compiled in 2014 by the VA, the federal government spent about $5,700 per veteran in Michigan, well below the U.S. average of $7,364 (VA, Office of Public Affairs, undated; VA, National Center for Veterans Analysis and Statistics, 2015; Burke, 2015). Over the same year, only about 22 percent of Michigan veterans used their health benefits, which is slightly lower than the national average of 27 percent.

The primary challenge that was reiterated in all the interviews and focus groups we conducted was a general lack of *awareness* of the benefits for which veterans were eligible. As one peacetime veteran noted, "I didn't know that I could go down to VA and get health care. I didn't know that they had accommodations down at the VA hospital that would help me . . . in getting jobs. I didn't even know that I was eligible for getting benefits because of my injury, a related service injury. You know, I didn't know any of this stuff until like within the last, what, two years?"

The fact that this veteran, who served in the Army roughly 30 years ago, went that long without any awareness of benefits was not a unique experience in our focus groups. A Gulf War veteran stated that "it's always been word of mouth since I've gotten out. . . . The way I found the Dearborn Vet Center—the only vet center that has meetings for Afghanistan and Iraqi vets—was going to the Detroit Vet Center and sitting in with Vietnam Era veterans, even some Korean War veterans, who didn't discuss the things that I needed to discuss. So it was just by chance."

Another veteran noted that "there's a lot of programs out there that are available. But . . . there's not a clearinghouse for all this stuff where a veteran can go to get a list of choices or options. I've found things just through research on my own . . . that I had no idea was out there." In fact, more than one veteran in our focus groups learned about certain benefits for the first time *during the focus groups.*

Others learned about programs and benefits in more challenging circumstances. For example, another veteran stated that "there are great programs out here. You just don't know s**t about them. And you don't need to spend one year or ten years in f*****g jail in order to find out what's going on, or you don't need to spend half your time in a mental hospital trying to figure out what's wrong with you. These things don't need to happen to anyone who sat out there in 140–150 f*****g degrees trying to fight a battle."

Even with general awareness of existing benefits, actually connecting veterans with these benefits was a challenge discussed across the stakeholder interviews and veteran focus groups we convened. The VA, which is the primary source of veteran benefits, manages separate processes for accessing health care, employment, education, housing, and financial support. As one of the federal government's largest bureaucracies, it operates hundreds of regional and state-level facilities and employs thousands across a wide range of occupations and sectors.

Consequently, veterans and their families must navigate the local and national rules, procedures, and personnel governing the VA to access care, receive benefits, file claims, and handle other business. Detroit area veterans indicated that this can be difficult. One Gulf War veteran said, "It is a process, but it isn't simple. And that's where your challenge is." Another veteran elaborated on this point, noting that "I was shot through the chest . . . It took me a year to get a benefit out of that because they needed documentation; they needed all these things—like, they do now, really? But I had to learn the system in order to get a benefit. It took me years and years to learn that system because I kept getting denied for all these things."

A peacetime veteran's perspective was that "the biggest thing about the health care was not knowing how to go about getting it. There was not anyone there to say, 'Hey, you know what? You need to go down here and see this person. You need to go down and take care of this or that.'" Furthermore, negative, initial experiences can adversely influence veterans' decisions to pursue care. For example, this same veteran noted that "that's one of the challenges, that, if a soldier hears about it [and] goes to the VA [and] his first experience is f****d up, then he ain't going back."

There are also logistical barriers that may prevent access to services even if a veteran can successfully navigate the VA system. One stakeholder we spoke with explained that "transportation is a big problem in Michigan, and especially in the Detroit area. There are some 250,000 veterans in Oakland, Macomb, and Wayne spread out over a lot of space. Not all of them have cars; especially the poor veterans can be without transportation. As a result, many are unable to get to a service provider or it may be too costly to do so." Public transportation is an issue in the metro Detroit region (Austin, 2015). A veteran without a car living in Rochester and using public transportation might spend two or two and a half hours to travel one way to the VA Medical Center in downtown Detroit, or an hour and a half to get to the Pontiac Vet Center. This may create a large time burden on any individual and could be a deterrent to seeking care. Stakeholders generally viewed transportation as a serious concern for veterans accessing benefits. One stakeholder posited that if "we remove . . . the limited location access and could [use] VA benefits anywhere, there would be a wave across the veteran community in seeking help." It should be noted that, in response to concerns over wait times at some VA facilities, Congress passed the VA Choice Act. In implementing this legislation, the VA began issuing Choice Cards to veterans in 2014 and expanded access to community-based sources of care for veterans who lived 40 miles or more from a center, allowing them to seek health care elsewhere.[1]

Many veterans with whom we spoke also felt that having civilian staff working in the VA was another challenge in connecting veterans with their benefits. A common sentiment was that "veterans don't want to talk with social workers and civilians because they feel that they can't identify." Others were blunter; as one veteran explained, "It takes a qualified person that has been in the military, whether they've been in combat or not." Another expressed his frustration, stating, "I don't really want a civilian telling me s**t about the military. I don't. Because you haven't hit ground. So, I could care less what you think and what you think that's wrong with me." A more moderate assessment was that while civilians working in VA facilities probably want to help, their general unfamiliarity with what being a veteran is really like creates an additional obstacle that prevents many veterans from accessing benefits.

Addressing Mental Health Problems

Put simply by one veteran with whom we spoke, "war is trauma." However, these veterans also thought that the extent of that trauma is often not fully recognized until the service member has left the combat zone and returned to civilian life. For many of the veterans we interviewed, years went by before they realized they suffered from mental health problems. Many reported experiencing grief, anger, depression, guilt,

---

[1] There are limited data available on the utilization of and satisfaction with the VA Choice program. Over time, it will be important to examine its impact on help-seeking behaviors.

hypervigilance, and loneliness. Some also reported relying upon alcohol to cope. One Gulf War veteran remarked, "I didn't know until somebody at the VA told me I was suffering from posttraumatic stress, I didn't know."

Veterans also described the negative perceptions and misperceptions surrounding mental health problems as being a challenge. One post-9/11 veteran suggested that the negative perceptions and attitudes toward mental health problems intensified as rank increased, saying, "The higher up you are, the less problems you are supposed to have." The presumption that officers or senior enlisted personnel should have fewer mental health challenges is a stereotype that this veteran believes prevents some veterans from receiving the appropriate level of care.

Another common theme expressed by the veterans with whom we spoke was that their families were not equipped to understand or help with their mental health problems. As one post-9/11 veteran stated, "They're not prepared for the issues that you have because there's no training for them. And there's no—like your mother, your father, they don't understand. And there's no education for them to understand. Especially if they're not computer literate. They can't go online and say, 'What's PTSD?' or whatever. They just want their son or daughter back the way they were." This lack of understanding leaves veterans feeling a lack of support from the individuals they most expect to be receiving it from.

Another issue veterans mentioned was the treatment of their mental health conditions. Some veterans expressed concern about the overreliance on medications, and the need to try several prescriptions before finding the right one. Several noted that this process left them both disappointed and frustrated. One veteran felt that the medical staff with whom he interacted had little empathy for the severity of his condition and the side effects of the many medications he took before finally landing on the appropriate intervention. Others indicated that, once they got into care, it was good and effective. However, the veterans that accessed services for mental health issues reported using a variety of sources, including Vet Centers, the VA medical centers, private mental health providers, and community mental health clinics. This raises issues about continuity of care and communication between all the different medical and mental health providers with whom the veterans are engaged.

Other veterans felt "stereotyped" by the VA and dismissed if their military occupational specialty (MOS) did not sound like a combat position. As one veteran put it, "That's one of the challenges that we have, that the VA doesn't recognize when they look at your MOS and they say—well, mine was easy, an infantry company commander and a chemical officer—'so, okay, you definitely was in the thick of things.' But when they look at a soldier that was a clerk, or 'you worked in the field doing things other than being a killer?' Yeah, okay, there's some questions there. And that may not have been all what that soldier did or got exposed to, or if he lost buddies . . . You're spending that much time in close quarters with one person or several people and you see them all the time and one ain't there no more, you stop and you start thinking, 'Who's next and how is it going to happen?' And so those soldiers, they didn't definitely have to be in the actual combat situation, they just had to be in the zone. And VA doesn't recognize that. They look at MOSs and they determine." This stereotyping could cause some veterans additional challenges in addressing their mental health issues, particularly if medical providers are not attuned to the possibility that they might exist.

Finding Meaningful Employment Opportunities

Many veterans noted that securing employment after military service is an important milestone for a veteran. Unfortunately, for many veterans with whom we spoke, adequate postservice employment took years to find. Veterans reported resorting to entry-level positions where they felt underemployed—that is, completing tasks below their experience level and income requirements. Moreover, unemployment and underemployment may lead to financial insecurity in the household, which may also place pressure on family relationships and ultimately the mental state of the veteran. It should be noted that these challenges are not limited to veterans. Despite recent improvements in local economic conditions (summarized in Chapter One), unemployment and underemployment in the metro Detroit area remain a concern for many community members, particularly among those whose skill sets better align with prior industries (e.g., automotive) than the newer industries that are growing in the region (e.g., technology).

Veterans described difficulty matching their service experience with such civilian credentials as college credit or occupational certification. During their service, some military personnel receive training and earn degrees in science or technology that translate directly to civilian credentials. However, after completing service, many veterans with whom we spoke noted that their only reputable degree was a high school diploma. Without credentials recognized by civilian employers, difficulty translating their MOS to a comparable civilian occupation, and a substantial period of time out of the civilian workforce, many veterans reported significant difficulty securing employment that reflected their professional experience. Some veterans also felt that some employers were reluctant to hire them due to concerns over mental health issues like PTSD.

Additionally, many veterans viewed local veteran job fairs as insufficient, stating that the opportunities presented were not diverse and often only included entry-level positions. As a veteran stated, "They need to be actually job fairs and not b******t things. Like, you go to a job fair and you find out they are only [hiring] truck drivers. . . . My undergrad is in chemistry and math; my master's is in environmental science. Why would I want to drive a truck for you, really? I'm not degrading anyone who drives a truck. But I'm just saying that if you're going to have a job fair, then tell us what it is. Don't just say, 'there's a job fair that's coming up.'" This dissatisfaction could reflect multiple shortcomings, from a regional shortage of the types of jobs in which veterans are interested to a lack of clear communication to potential attendees about the types of employers that will be participating in each job fair, and the positions for which they are hiring. For the veteran, however, the outcome is the same: a challenge in finding meaningful employment opportunities.

Conclusion

During our organized discussions, Detroit area veterans reflected on several challenges related to the transition from military service to civilian life. Perhaps foremost among them was a lack of awareness about the support, assistance, and benefits provided by the VA. The veterans with whom we spoke generally felt as though there were many good resources available, but that there was no centralized way to learn about the programs that were available or for which they were eligible. These veterans also agreed that extra effort was often necessary, such as working with a veteran service officer and filing appeals, to secure the financial and medical benefits available for them.

Veterans also noted that, despite national and local initiatives to hire veterans, it could be difficult securing the types of jobs they wanted and for which they felt they were qualified. Factors included credentialing, uncertainty about how and where their military experience would be valued by civilian employers, and dissatisfaction with the types of available jobs presented at job fairs for veterans. These challenges hindered their general ability both to adjust back to civilian life and to effectively deal with their mental health challenges.

Across our focus groups and interviews, veterans also reflected on the negative effects that mental illness had on their personal relationships and their overall livelihood. Several veterans stated they languished in poor mental health and poverty for many years before taking advantage of their eligible benefits and mental health supports.

Readers familiar with the literature will note that the issues and challenges discussed by the veterans in the metro Detroit area with whom we spoke are similar to those expressed by service members and veterans from other communities.[2] While the challenges are not unique to veterans in metro Detroit and the surrounding communities, the specific support services and resources available to these veterans are often state- and county-based resources or nongovernmental resources tailored to meet the needs of these veterans. In the next chapter, we discuss the services and resources available within the region in more detail.

---

[2] For examples, see Castro, Kintzle, and Hassan (2015) and Carter and Kidder (2013). These examples are not limited to U.S. veterans; Bashford et al. (2015) offers perspectives of veterans and their family members in England.

CHAPTER FOUR

Available Mental Health Support Services and Resources

There are a variety of organizations in the metro Detroit area that make mental health services and support available to veterans. Some of these organizations and resources target veterans specifically, while others are available to all individuals living in the region regardless of their veteran status. The types of programs and services available could be summarized in a number of ways: by sector (government or nongovernment), by geographic location, by eligibility criteria, or by other organizing frameworks. Mental health services and resources are offered by federal, state, and county government agencies, as well as nongovernmental organizations. However, veteran access to these services often depends on the specific eligibility criteria defined by the service provider. Many times, eligibility is determined based upon the characteristics of military service and the individual's discharge status.[1] As a result, from a veteran's perspective, service organizations may fall into two categories: those available to veterans who qualify based on certain eligibility requirements, and those available to all veterans regardless of their status.

We discuss the types of services and supports for veterans with mental health problems within these two categories. What is discussed here is by no means an exhaustive list of all services and supports available to veterans or community members with mental health problems in the metro Detroit area. Rather, the services and resources in the

---

[1] For example, see Szymendera (2015) for a discussion of veteran eligibility requirements.

region mentioned here represent the types of organizations working with the veteran community and on issues of mental health. (For a more illustrative list of organizations that serve veterans in the metro Detroit region please see the appendix.)

Services and Resources Available to Eligible Veterans

Title 38 of the U.S. Code (Section 101) specifies that to be eligible for federal benefits and services for veterans, an individual must meet certain criteria. Typically, these criteria require that the person have active U.S. military service for a minimum period of time, generally the lesser of the full period ordered to active duty or 24 months, and be discharged "under conditions other than dishonorable." We provide a brief overview of the services and programs available specifically to individuals who meet criteria specified by federal statute.

Department of Veterans Affairs

The VA provides a wide array of benefits and services for eligible veterans, including furnishing health care services to veterans enrolled in their health care system. Currently, the VA health care system is organized into 21 veteran integrated service networks (VISN). Michigan is part of VISN 11, along with Indiana and Illinois. Michigan is home to five VA Medical Centers, located in Saginaw, Battle Creek, Ann Arbor, Iron Mountain, and Detroit. In addition, there are 22 community-based outpatient clinics and eight vet centers across the state (see Figure 4.1). Several of these facilities fall within the metro Detroit area (see Figure 4.2); we describe these further.

The John D. Dingell VA Medical Center in Detroit is the largest provider of mental health care services for veterans in the metro Detroit area. It is composed of a number of programs dedicated to issues of mental health, including acute psychiatric services, primary-care mental health integration, mental health intake service, a general mental health clinic, SUD services, a PTSD clinical team, psychosocial rehabilitation and recovery center, neuropsychology/diagnostics, mental health residential recovery treatment program, military sexual

Figure 4.1
Department of Veteran Affairs Health Facilities in Michigan

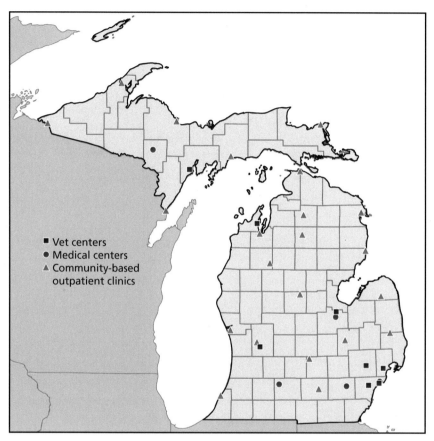

- ■ Vet centers
- ● Medical centers
- ▲ Community-based
  outpatient clinics

trauma, and a homeless program. These programs provide psychiatric attention, inpatient beds, comprehensive psychosocial assessment, residential treatment for homeless veterans with mental health issues, psychopharmacological services, and more services that are available to veterans who received a discharge status of honorable, under honorable conditions, or general.

The VA Medical Center is located in downtown Detroit and also has satellite clinics and centers throughout the counties surrounding

Figure 4.2
Department of Veteran Affairs Health Facilities in Metro Detroit Area

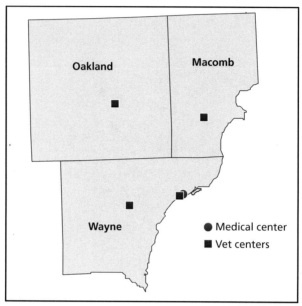

the metro Detroit area (see Figure 4.1). However, these satellite locations may not offer the full suite of mental health services available downtown. The Pontiac Vet Clinic offers tele-health mental health services, whereby the veteran can receive one-on-one counseling with a nurse practitioner and doctor who are located in a different location through the use of a video technology platform. The clinic also runs a PTSD group counseling session once a week. Aside from the clinic, there are four vet centers located in Dearborn, Detroit (which is in very close proximity to the Medical Center), Macomb County, and Pontiac (the Pontiac Vet Center is in the Pontiac Vet Clinic). Vet centers offer counseling services to veterans with mental health needs. They provide one-on-one as well as group counseling services and family support counseling.

State-Based and Funded Resources for Eligible Veterans

Almost all states in the United States have an agency or designated office that administers benefits and programs for eligible veterans. As such, Michigan, like many other states, operates or funds several programs that offer financial benefits and support services to their resident veterans. At the state level, the MVAA is housed within the Michigan Department of Military and Veteran Affairs and works to decrease barriers and increase access to education, employment, health care, and quality of life for eligible veterans residing in Michigan. Its website offers several resources about benefits and services available for veterans throughout the state, including tools and resources for job seekers and those in need of emergency assistance. Veterans can use the website or contact MVAA through at 1-800-MICH-VET.

In discussions and interviews, MVAA leadership described a strong need for service providers to increase their interconnectedness and better implement referrals, wraparound services, and warm handoffs. As such, they identified a major objective of the MVAA as building "that collaborative environment at the community level so the community is empowered to take ownership but they know there is higher-level support." A major part of this effort has been the introduction of VCATs in Michigan, building and maintaining a portfolio of service providers across the state, and a partnership with the 211 help line to direct veterans to veteran-specific organizations.

The MVAA is also involved in serving veterans directly through the Michigan Veterans Trust Fund (MVTF) and advocating for veterans through efforts to change state legislation. With respect to offering mental health support, the MVAA is running a program through the MVTF that pays for up to five community mental health service provider visits for a veteran who is eligible for federal benefits but not currently registered in the VA health care system. This allows veterans to receive needed services without delay while applying or registering for federal benefits. However, eligibility for MVTF funding (like those provided by the federal VA) requires an honorable discharge, as well as at least 180 days of service during a period of war. Peacetime veterans, as well as those with a less than honorable discharge status, are not eligible for this support. The MVAA is also working to amend the Michigan Mental Health Code to include veterans as a priority population and have "mental health care" explicitly mentioned in the qualifying reasons for undue hardship funds from the MVTF that are provided to veterans for housing, hospitalization, food, fuel, clothing, and medical services not obtainable elsewhere.

County-Based Services and Resources for Eligible Veterans

Each of the three counties that compose the metro Detroit area (Macomb, Oakland, and Wayne) have county-level veteran affairs departments that facilitate access to federal and state benefits to veterans who reside within the county.[2] Their staffing varies from six to 12 counselors (not including adjunct staff). The size of the staff does dictate both the types and amount of services they can provide. Wayne County Veterans Affairs, with the smallest staff of the three counties, focuses on financial hardship issues and targets honorably discharged veterans who are eligible for local and MVTF-funded aid. As such, it mainly provides rent and utility assistance to returning veterans and limits assistance to once every year or two. Veterans with issues that cannot be served directly are referred to federal VA services or local community providers.

In Macomb and Oakland, the primary role of the county veteran services counselors is to assist veterans and their families applying for federal, state, and county benefits. This includes securing supporting documentation, submitting applications, and handling appeals for medical, educational, and burial benefits. In regard to mental health, as one county veterans affairs director said, "Ninety percent of what we do is give them referral information and encouragement to get care." Veterans with mental health–related needs are commonly referred to local vet centers or the VA medical center in Detroit. However, there is no follow-up to ensure that care was received or that the veteran did

---

[2] These services are typically available to veterans who qualify for VA benefits based on their discharge status. Veterans with "other than honorable" or "dishonorable" may not be able to receive services or resources from VA, federal, state, or local agencies, increasing the strain they may put on local communities and creating opportunities for nongovernmental agencies to intervene. For more information, see 38 U.S.C. § 101, "Definitions," and Carter (2013).

connect with the center. The county directors we spoke to reported that they will work with any veteran who walks through their door (regardless of their eligibility status) but the services they can actually provide are limited by each veteran's eligibility status based upon federal and state criteria. However, the Oakland County office also reported working with four veteran treatment courts to help veterans navigate benefits eligibility and access to support services.

Services from Nongovernmental Sources

There are a number of other support organizations in the metro Detroit area that run programs specifically designed to serve veterans. Most of the large traditional veteran service organizations, such as American Legion and Veterans of Foreign Wars (VFW) have posts throughout the region. There are also active chapters of newer organizations, such as Student Veterans of America; Team Red, White, and Blue; Team Rubicon; and the Mission Continues. These organizations are primarily designed to help connect veterans to each other and share information about benefits and services to support veterans living in the community. There are also several general support programs available to veterans and military families, through individual Guard and Reserve units located in the region, as well as those hosted by the University of Michigan's Military Support Programs and Networks. None of them offers clinical mental health services directly; however, most do offer referrals to other service providers in the region who can deliver direct mental health services and support to veterans. The level of service or direct resources provided by these organization to veterans in the region may vary upon eligibility criteria, some may require "proof" of military service or impose other restrictions on benefits (e.g., veterans service organizations can only help VA-eligible veterans apply for federal benefits).

In addition, other nongovernmental, nonprofit organizations in the region target veterans through specific programs. One such program, "Operation Good Jobs," run by Goodwill in Detroit, provides services to veterans and their families to aid in employment-related problems. The program's direct services include career planning and navigation, finding employment, retention strategies, and a financial literacy program with the Bank of America. Like the government-sponsored programs listed above, Operation Good Jobs does not serve veterans with dishonorable discharges. While this program does not provide any mental health–related services directly, they reported making a number of referrals for veterans with mental health issues to partner organizations.

In addition to the Goodwill program, a handful of other nongovernmental and community-based organizations in the metro Detroit area have been awarded Supportive Services for Veteran Families (SSVF) Grants, which are aimed at improving housing stability among very low-income veteran families. Volunteers of America (VOA), a national organization with a strong presence in Michigan and the Detroit region, is a recipient of the SSVF grant from the VA. Because it is a federally supported program, the SSVF grant money is only available to support veterans with an honorable discharge and who were on orders for a mission for at least 24 hours. The VOA also provides employment training programs for homeless or unemployed veterans that include case management, resume building, counseling, and job placement. It does not provide direct clinical mental health services to veterans but will work to connect eligible veterans to mental health programs available through the VA Medical Center.

Services and Resources Available to All Veterans

As we discussed above, the majority of services targeted specifically for veterans in the region limit access to such services and benefits to only those that meet certain eligibility requirements. This often leaves several veterans with mental health problems with few choices for support services. However, there are a number of organizations that function on a local level to support veterans in their communities in a variety of ways, regardless of discharge status.

One such organization, the Grosse Pointe War Memorial (GPWM), does not have a specific area of focus such as mental health, but works to serve the current needs of the local veteran community. The GPWM began as an organization dedicated to honoring veterans through Memorial Day services, Veterans Day breakfasts, and other events in the community. However, GPWM leaders came to recognize that much more was needed in their community and said that today they seek to be "leaders of thought as well as leaders of action when it comes to serving veterans." An organization like the GPWM may be well positioned at the intersection of local veterans and service providers; while it does not provide direct services like a community mental health (CMH) clinic, it works with veterans and service providers to facilitate care in the community. Importantly, GPWM also works with veterans to identify current issues and is able to direct efforts toward addressing these pressing problems. Leaders said they are "trying to smooth the way home for service personnel separating from service," as they have identified this as a need in the community. The GPWM and similar organizations have the potential to be incredibly powerful facilitators for veterans to access services and for understanding the current needs of local veteran communities.

Veterans with mental health problems, like other residents in the region, also may seek services from private providers or community mental health clinics. However, their access to such services may be restricted based upon other factors, such as health care coverage or specific condition. We provide some information about mental health services in the metro Detroit region for all veterans, regardless of their service characteristics or discharge status.

Community-Based Mental Health Service Providers

Like most communities, there are a number of individual mental health service providers (e.g., psychiatrists, psychologists, social workers, marriage therapists) in the metro Detroit area that offer mental health care. These individuals may be affiliated with large health systems (e.g., Henry Ford Health System), work in private health clinics, or operate solo office practices. Over the past few years, there have been several attempts to raise awareness of veteran mental health issues among community-based mental health providers and to create specific registries of local providers that can serve the veteran population. We describe two such efforts in the metro Detroit area.

GaH, a national organization with a large presence in the metro Detroit area, is a network of clinicians who volunteer their time to support the mental health needs of returning veterans. While its initial priority was to serve post-9/11 veterans, GaH reports that their providers will not turn any veteran or veteran affiliated loved one away. There are around 230–240 participating clinicians in Michigan with about 100 of those in the Detroit area. To participate in GaH, a licensed or certified clinician must agree to volunteer one free hour of services per week in support of veteran mental health treatment or raising awareness. Local GaH leadership reported also attending outreach events, providing training, and performing annual vetting of member clinicians by checking licenses and practice status. Veterans can self-identify and call member clinicians directly or call GaH for assistance in finding a clinician. Veterans or family members can find clinicians in their region on the GaH website. As a member of the VCAT, GaH also hopes to receive referrals from other organizations that work with veterans.

Star Behavioral Health Providers (SBHP) is a network of clinicians who have received specialized training to work with military veterans and their families. Hosted by Michigan State University and other collaborators, the SBHP offers three tiers of training for community-based providers. The first tier includes training on military culture and the challenges that go along with military service to clinicians, as well as community members. In tiers two and three, it offers additional clinical skills training for licensed mental health providers that focus on addressing veterans with behavioral/mental health issues with specific evidence-based approaches. Clinicians that complete the training are entered into SBHP's registry of certified clinicians that is accessible to veterans seeking services. This registry is intended to serve as a referral resource for the Michigan National Guard, but it is also publicly accessible, similar to GaH. One issue that the local SBHP leadership reported that it hopes to address is the poor uptake rate of veterans who are connected to service providers. The Michigan SBHP program coordinator states that matching a veteran to a service provider can be difficult and there is only about a 50/50 chance of success. An unsuccessful first contact can sour a veteran's perception of all mental health service providers. Therefore, SBHP's training focuses on providing cultural and contextual education, along with clinical skills, so that clinicians in the network are better able to relate to and work with veterans. Once connected to a SBHP provider, the veteran and provider are responsible for working out how the services will be covered. SBHP, unlike GaH, does not expect the providers to offer their services free of charge. However, many may offer sliding scale fees or work with the veteran's health care insurance agency to provide access to services.

Community-Based Mental Health Agencies

In most counties throughout the United States, there are community mental health agencies. The Detroit Wayne Mental Health Authority (DWMHA) is a public mental health system operating in Detroit and Wayne County. It is funded primarily through Medicaid at approximately $650 million, and its broad network of services reaches around 100,000 individuals annually. DWMHA currently functions by contracting five managers of comprehensive provider networks (MCPNs), who, in turn, contract with more than 80 service providers, hospitals, and local organizations. Its target population consists of adults and children with serious mental illness issues, as well as those with SUDs. While the state has identified veterans as a priority population within this group, DWMHA does not receive any funding specifically for veterans and often relies on veterans' own eligibility for VA services or other services covered by their insurance. In 2015, the service providers, hospitals, and local organizations within the DWMHA network served 198 self-identifying veterans. Thus, veterans make up less than 1 percent of the persons served by DWMHA each year despite its large network of care.

The surrounding counties of Oakland, Macomb, and St. Clair also have community mental health agencies/authorities that serve adults with mental illness, developmental disorders, SUDs, and children with emotional disorders. They provide some outpatient services in Macomb and St. Clair, such as Assertive Community Treatment (ACT), psychotherapy, mental health counseling, and SUD counseling and support. Like DWMHA, most of the funding for these services comes through Medicaid. When serving veterans eligible for VA benefits, county community mental health organizations will seek reimbursement from the VA.

Some county mental health authorities (CMHAs) have partnered with local service providers that have been awarded an SSVF grant. There were seven such organizations operating in the metro Detroit area for the 2014 fiscal year, but only two awardees across all of Michigan for the 2015 fiscal year.[3]

Mental Health Advocacy

Along with community service providers, there are advocacy organizations that work on policy and awareness issues across state and regional levels. The Mental Health Association in Michigan is a state affiliate of Mental Health America that analyzes and advocates public policy for all those with mental illness. The main issues it currently focuses on in Michigan are access to medications, access to treatments, access to housing, and monitoring those incarcerated with mental illness, including veterans. The National Alliance on Mental Illness (NAMI) is a national grass-roots organization that engages in advocacy on issues of mental illness, as well as education and community outreach. NAMI runs a number of educational programs that target family members and caregivers of those with mental health issues and even have a couple of programs that target veterans. Their national "Family-to-Family" service is a 12-week program run twice a year at the VA Hospital for veteran family members. NAMI Homefront is a new six-week adaptation of the "Family-to-Family" program specific for military and veteran families that is also now available at no cost in Michigan. Alongside these programs, NAMI offers family support groups at ten locations throughout the metro Detroit area, a helpline, and advocacy efforts that engage medical students and legislative issues.

---

[3] The 2014 recipients were Wayne Metropolitan Community Action Agency, Bluewater Center for Independent Living, Training & Treatment Innovations, Inc., Oakland Livingston Human Services Agency, Wayne County Neighborhood Legal Services, Volunteers of America, and Community Action Partnership. The 2015 recipients are Volunteers of America and Alger Marquette Community Action Board.

Supportive Housing and Wraparound Services

Permanent housing for homeless veterans is a newer development in veterans' services in the Detroit area. Since many veterans who experience homelessness also experience mental health–related problems, these housing programs may serve an important role in addressing the mental health needs of veterans. Piquette Square, operated by Southwest Solutions, is a 150-unit residence exclusively for homeless veterans. Along with permanent housing, Piquette also offers wraparound services, including workforce training, adult literacy, financial counseling, and mental health counseling; all of these services are provided on site. While Piquette is open to any veteran regardless of discharge status, status may affect eligibility for some of these wraparound services, such as Southwest Solutions' workforce development training. The workforce training is aimed at socializing veterans into the world of work and often in collaboration with an employer looking to fill a specific job. While Piquette is not a clinical treatment facility and residents are not required to participate in any of these services, the president of Southwest Solutions pointed out that, "if you make services available and start with building a relationship with [veterans] so they feel comfortable recognizing the help they need, then you create a system of care for those individuals." As a part of this effort, Southwest Solutions is working to fund a peer-to-peer drop-in center where veterans can talk with other veterans about issues and needs.

The Piquette Square project was unique among the stakeholders we spoke with in that it provided a wide array of services at one location. However, a couple of the stakeholders we talked to expressed concern for centralized homeless housing. As one stakeholder put it, ". . . services should be available where [veterans] are already and not where the building is convenient." This is similar to concerns related to centralized care regarding the VA Medical center discussed in Chapter Three.

Making Connections in the Veteran Support Landscape

As we have outlined, there are many different organizations and service providers in the region that offer services to veterans with mental health problems, whether it be support to receive financial benefits or the provision of direct clinical services. However, these organizations and entities function largely independently of each other and may be spread out across the region. In 2013, the MVAA contracted the Altarum Institute to implement the VCAT model in Michigan's Region 10 (Wayne, Macomb, and Oakland counties). The VCAT's intended purpose is to drive community collaboration around the provision of veteran resources and services. It does so by convening service providers throughout the region organized around four pillars: education, employment, health, and quality of life. At the time of this study, there were 391 members representing 237 organizations that ranged from veteran-specific service providers to CMHA providers, including even some networks of mental health providers, like GaH. There are no specific criteria for organizations that seek VCAT membership and the VCAT itself does not provide any services directly to veterans; rather it aims to connect service providers to each other (through regular meetings/gatherings). However, VCAT local leaders reported that they are hoping to implement an online system intended to facilitate warm hand-offs of veterans between service providers. We spoke with many stakeholders about their connections and awareness of other veteran service providers: Some were familiar with the VCAT meetings; others were not. Of those that had participated in some of the meetings, some noted remaining concerns about creating more meaningful connections across the service provider landscape and ensuring better referrals for veterans beyond just sitting together at meetings.

Perceived Gaps in the Service Landscape

While many of the organizations we spoke with reported that there were ample services available for veterans in the region, they also noted several challenges in ensuring that all veterans got the care they needed, including lack of awareness of resources among veterans, federally imposed eligibility requirements, funding limitations, capacity constraints, and the lack of connection or integration among service providers and with the veteran community.

Stakeholders noted a perception that most veterans in the region lacked an awareness of the benefits and resources available to support their mental health problems. At the same time, many noted a concern about the lack of information about veterans living in the region, which hampered their organization's ability to conduct outreach. Further, the restrictions based upon an individual meeting certain eligibility requirements often limited some agencies' abilities to meet the population's needs. Thus, these eligibility requirements may pose an important barrier to getting help. As was outlined above, any veteran with a dishonorable discharge, regardless of length of service, is not eligible for federally sponsored veteran benefits. This can be problematic because, as one stakeholder pointed out, "the activity that caused your less-than-honorable discharge could have been brought on by what you experienced during service." In these cases, veterans may try to seek out support but be told repeatedly that they are not eligible and either give up or be left to find a nonveteran-specific community provider.

Other stakeholders noted concerns about the restrictions on both the amount of funds they receive to support veterans and the restrictions placed upon the use of the funds. For example, one stakeholder noted, "a big challenge is that most of the dollars we receive for veterans come with restrictions. . . . Some people say, 'here's a grant for workforce development.' Well great, but will that allow for literacy coaching or getting a vehicle to get to their job? Having unrestricted dollars is a huge need." Removing some of these restrictions on dollars for veterans may open up opportunities for local organizations to better serve their veteran communities. Other organizations garner local funding to support their work. However, this may also be problematic; as one representative stated, "we have mandates from the state to ensure serving veterans are a high priority population, but the majority of funding goes to the VA, so they get the gold and we get the shaft . . . we will look at ways to maximize and stretch additional funding sources but oftentimes what gives is the quality of care."

Funding and reimbursement rates were also a potential barrier to delivering services to veterans. For example, representatives from CMHA noted that the VA reimbursement often does not cover the full cost of care, requiring the agency to draw upon the general fund. We spoke with one CMHA representative who said the agency is severely restricted in the amount and type of services that can be offered to veterans, especially those who are VA eligible, due to this extra cost burden. The CMHA even stopped sending providers to the in-state SBHP training (described above) because they would not be able to serve enough veterans to make it worthwhile.

Some of the CMH organizations with whom we spoke refer veterans to vet centers for counseling, but reported that they often hear that the centers are overbooked. In one scenario, a vet center opened with three counselors and was fully booked within days. A CMH stakeholder indicated that, "I think how they handle it is by putting people though the group sessions," which the stakeholder indicated might not be appropriate for many cases that need one-on-one counseling. Some community stakeholders reported that this high demand at vet centers for counseling is a result of the demand for local and convenient access to mental health services that is not sufficiently addressed.

Stakeholders revealed a tension between the desire to provide community-based services and aid to veterans and the reality of the current service landscape that tends toward centralized services (like the VA Medical Center model). In some cases, like Piquette, when trying to provide wraparound services, the costs associated with a diffuse network of sites are prohibitive because each location would have to provide each service. It seems likely that overcoming this issue across the region and stakeholder community will involve a larger effort of coordination and integration on the part of service providers throughout the area, well beyond what is being accomplished through the current VCAT meetings.

Conclusion

Discussions with stakeholders revealed a wide array of support organizations and service providers that work on issues of mental health and veterans with mental health needs. Within the region, there are dedicated federal and state resources that serve veterans through government organizations and grants, local organizations and programs aimed directly at veterans, and community services and advocacy groups that work on mental health issues for the entire population. However, just having a large number and variety of organizations devoted to issues of mental health (see the appendix) does not ensure coordination, quality, accessibility, or a paucity of gaps in services. Nor does it prevent other barriers to obtaining mental health services. Our discussions with stakeholders and local veterans shed light on many of the remaining roadblocks that veterans and others in the area may face in obtaining the mental health services they need. These included issues around awareness, access, and capacity.

CHAPTER FIVE

Observed Gaps and Recommendations for Improving Support

As described in the previous chapter, we identified a number of resources for metro Detroit area veterans with mental health problems. In fact, most with whom we spoke noted that there were many resources in the region. However, stakeholders and veterans also pointed to some gaps in the service and support landscape that may lead to unmet mental health needs among veterans in the metro Detroit region. These issues span multiple domains, including challenges associated with ensuring early identification of problems and awareness of resources, facilitating access to high quality treatment, and coordination and integration of services. Below, we describe each of these issues in more detail and provide a series of recommendations on how to close these gaps.

Connecting Veterans to Resources

Despite the availability of a range of resources available to support veterans with mental health problems, stakeholders pointed to several specific barriers to veterans accessing these services. The first was the veteran's ability to recognize they may need help and be willing to reach out for services. The second was related to the veteran being aware of and eligible for the available resources to access the help when needed. A third barrier noted by stakeholders was that organizations with resources often were not connected directly to the veteran population. A fourth barrier reported was the capacity of the organizations to serve veterans within a reasonable time frame and in ways that best meet the needs of the veterans they serve.

Recognizing Help Is Needed

For veterans, the transition to civilian life can be abrupt and unsettling as they try to readjust to a new normal. Over the past several years, the U.S. Department of Defense has expanded the availability of transition assistance programs that serve to facilitate employment transitions and enable registration for VA benefits in an effort to smooth this transition. Still, many veterans leave military service with service-related mental health problems, whereas others may develop mental health problems later in life. Veterans and stakeholders that we spoke to noted that many veterans often have to "hit the bottom" after transitioning from military service before they reach out for help, or before someone else recognizes that they need help. Some veterans noted that they were referred for mental health care when they applied for housing support, legal assistance, or job placement, indicating that perhaps liaison staff were the first to identify a potential mental health need. Veterans, however, noted frustration over not being offered this assistance earlier, noting that they didn't recognize their own needs and getting help earlier might have prevented some of the years of hardship they endured. For some veterans, other life events may trigger the recognition of need, like retirement or relationship changes (divorce, death of a spouse, remarriage). The recognition of need may come across the life span and at varying times after separating from military service. As such, programs that focus on just the young cohort of veterans currently transitioning from military service may fail to include veterans who separated years prior but are still facing problems and need assistance. Similarly, awareness programs or efforts that rely heavily upon the more-traditional veteran service organizations (membership-based groups) may miss those veterans not connected or not interested in joining.

Finding Help and Accessing Care

Once there is recognition of needing mental health support, challenges persist for veterans if information about available resources and programs is difficult to find and restricted to specific groups of veterans. Although there are numerous pathways by which individuals may find out about mental health services, the majority rely on existing connections to other services or resources and on understanding eligibility requirements, which are often quite complex. Within each county, for example, the county veteran service officer often serves as the important "navigator" not only for benefits, but also for referrals to sources of mental health treatment from the VA and other community-based resources, including private providers. While veteran service officers can often be important subject matter experts to help veterans understand and apply for benefits, not all veterans get connected with these veteran service officers early, nor are all veterans eligible for such programs and services.

Many veterans rely upon word of mouth from friends or coworkers, or other veterans. Veteran service organizations like the American Legion, VFW, and even the Michigan Buddy-to-Buddy, use peer-based approaches to offer support, camaraderie, and word-of-mouth referrals, but can only do so for the veterans who connect with them. Employers also may become a source of information and resources through Employee Assistance Programs. For veterans returning to college campuses, their local campus organizations can become important resources as well.

Despite these resources, within the metro Detroit area, there is not a unified, centralized resource that will provide information about potential services to interested veterans regardless of eligibility status. While the MVAA website does provide a listing of resources and offers links to many service providers, those services are often restricted to only those who are VA-eligible.

Much of the awareness around potential services also can be affected by whether information is made available to veterans at critical time points, such as their transition to civilian life, or as they reach out for other sources of support (e.g., employment opportunities, housing support). Veterans noted that, even once aware of resources and services, knowing what you are eligible to receive can be confusing, suggesting that additional resources are needed to help veterans navigate this additional step of eligibility determination.

Moving forward, it is essential that, in all of these settings, not only are the coordinators, leaders, or managers aware of the potential mental health issues that veterans may face, they also must know how to connect veterans to needed services through referrals or introductions to appropriate, high-quality service providers. Many noted, however, that the proximity of the services available in relation to the veteran can be a challenge. For example, travel distance and other transportation difficulties were noted barriers for some in accessing available VA mental health resources. As such, even if services were identified, they were not always a feasible long-term solution to obtaining care.

For those that are not VA-eligible (such as some members of the National Guard and Reserve), or those that were other than honorably discharged from military service, finding services for which they are eligible can be even more challenging. Re-examining, updating, and publicizing the eligibility criteria for various organizations and service providers may be necessary to ensure that these veterans have access to needed mental health care in the region. While these individuals are able to use their community-based mental health agencies or private providers (such as those through GaH), resource or capacity constraints may limit the ability of those organizations to serve all veterans with needs. Clearly publicizing the existing eligibility criteria is a first step to ensuring that veterans are channeled to the services for which they are eligible. If resource or capacity constraints on existing services result in excess demand by veterans ineligible for other programs, this argues for the need for additional resources in this area.

Connecting to Veterans

Many stakeholders reported frustration in not knowing where the veterans are and thus being unable to reach out and inform them of services that may be available, or offer assistance to those most in need. A few stakeholders noted the inability to obtain contact information for the veterans residing in the region. Some have tried mailing campaigns and have hosted events that were advertised publicly to bring veterans in and raise awareness of available benefits and resources. However, novel approaches may be needed to push the information out to veterans in multiple ways—such as through employers, health care providers, college campuses, and nonveteran social service agencies—to ensure that information is available to veterans as they interact in other settings as well.

Organizational Capacity to Serve Veterans

A final challenge noted by some service providers was one of capacity. Some reflected that even when they had a veteran with a mental health need within their population and they could identify an organization that could provide the necessary services, veterans may experience long wait times before being seen by the other organization's providers because the organization had limited staff or a limited number of program slots available. This lack of staffing or program capacity can be frustrating for both the veteran and the referring organization. This was particularly a concern for those making referrals to the local vet centers. This observation suggests that there may be a need to increase the number of providers available within the vet center to ensure that veterans can be served within a reasonable time frame within that setting. A second challenge associated with resource capacity had to do with restrictions on the financial resources available to compensate providers or organizations for their services. This came in two forms—the restrictions on the use of the state block funds by the CMHAs and the VA reimbursement rates for services provided in the community. These resource constraints may be having a negative impact on the willingness of available providers in the region to serve the population, as some of our stakeholders noted a decision to stop serving veterans because it did not make financial sense.

Recommendations

We identified a number of recommendations that could serve to address the gaps outlined above. To fully address the gaps and create a comprehensive approach, stakeholders in the metro Detroit area will need to pursue all of these actions in concert to ensure sustainable and effective solutions. Simply attending to one area (such as raising awareness) may not close the gap by itself within the region. Thus, we recommend a comprehensive approach to implementing these recommendations.

Raising Awareness

Building a community that is more aware and that is willing to take action to improve the lives of veterans will require multiple efforts to educate, inform, and motivate individuals (veterans and nonveterans), organizations, and service providers. Often, public education or awareness campaigns are implemented to disseminate information through multiple channels with a specific goal of raising awareness. However, to ensure the information is utilized and acted upon often requires that these campaigns build efforts beyond just "spreading the word" about available services.

Crafting and implementing successful public awareness campaigns has the potential benefit of educating stakeholders, dispelling myths, and facilitating behavior change. There are several examples of successful campaigns that have raised awareness of a particular public health concern and motivated community engagement, including efforts to improve awareness of mental health issues among youth (e.g., *In One Voice*), increase organ donation among minorities, and increase healthy behaviors among older adults (Callender and Miles, 2010; Livingston et al., 2013; Reger et al., 2002). As such, there are multiple potential insights that can be garnered and applied to crafting specific campaigns related to veteran mental health in the Detroit region.

Multiple stakeholders can benefit from such approaches to improve how veterans with mental health problems are identified and referred to appropriate care when needed. To improve awareness within the Detroit region, three specific audiences could be targeted with such approaches: veterans, community-based health care providers, and other social service providers. While some awareness-building efforts have been conducted to date, prior research indicates that sustained efforts are often needed to support the implementation of new behaviors among the target population or in the specified environment.

Empowering Veterans

Many former service personnel transition from military life and do not identify themselves as a veteran, nor do they come forward asking for specific benefits or services. However, some may find themselves in need of assistance at some point in the future and be unaware of the many resources or programs available. Thus, sustained efforts to disseminate information and raise awareness of available services are essential. Organizations that provide benefits and services will need to evaluate the best mechanisms for reaching veterans continually, not only as they transition from military service, but also at other times across their lifespan. It may be particularly challenging to reach veterans already in the community and not connected to services. Coordinated outreach efforts across stakeholders and service providers may improve efficiency and effectiveness of these educational campaigns. While the MVAA has worked with the regional 211 line and the VCATs to publicize the availability of veterans' benefits through traditional and social media, as well as through town hall meetings and community events, there may be additional opportunities to ensure that these messages are consistently shared. Reaching out to some of the organizations to engage them in outreach and awareness efforts may also help to reach additional veterans. In some cities (e.g., Boston, Chicago, Atlanta), partnerships with local professional sports organizations and large employer organizations have been helpful in raising awareness of veteran mental health issues and promoting service-seeking, as have community-gathering opportunities. Service providers in the Detroit region could work in innovative ways to ensure that resources for veterans are distributed through local business networks, the Detroit international auto show at Cobo Hall, or sporting events (Tigers, Lions, Red Wings, and Pistons).

Training Community-Based Health Care Providers

While training opportunities exist to promote military cultural competence among existing mental health providers within Michigan and to create registries of available mental health resources, more efforts are likely needed to raise awareness of veteran's mental health issues among health care providers outside of mental health care circles, as well as to ensure that providers are trained in the appropriate evidence-based approaches. Veterans with mental health problems may be present in other health care settings (primary or specialty care) and ensuring that all health care providers take an appropriate military and trauma-related history can facilitate the identification of unmet mental health needs and perhaps facilitate referral and treatment seeking. The American Academy of Nursing (undated) implemented the "Have You Ever Served?" campaign in 2014 as a means of promoting greater awareness among nursing professionals. As part of the Joining Forces Initiative, the American Association of Medical College similarly made a pledge to engage medical schools in training the future physician workforce on the special issues affecting military and veteran populations. However, specific training and education campaigns could be implemented within non-VA health care systems and provider groups in the metro Detroit region (e.g., Henry Ford Health System).

Educating Social Service Providers

Several veterans that we interviewed had experience accessing services and benefits through other social service agencies in the governmental and nongovernmental sectors. Veterans described varying experiences with these organizations and agencies, with some asking about military history and others not. Identifying veterans and military-affiliated individuals may help ensure that veterans can be referred to other programs and benefits for which they may be eligible, including mental health care. Military cultural awareness training programs for other serving professionals (including employers, lawyers, law enforcement personnel, etc.) are available;[1] however, beyond raising awareness about military and veteran culture, these professionals may need additional education and support to understand how to assess military affiliation, as well as information about available programs and resources for veterans in order to make appropriate referrals.

Creating Connections

A recurrent theme in our discussions with stakeholders and veterans was the apparent disconnect between the resources available and the veterans with potential needs. Some reflected great frustration with the time and energy it took to learn about available services and benefits,

---

[1] PsychArmor (www.psycharmor.org) is just one entity that provides training for non–health care providers on how to work effectively with veterans. Its courses are available at no cost and while it could provide the foundation for increasing the sensitivity among social service providers, additional information may be needed to ensure that providers refer veterans to the appropriate, local resources for additional assistance when warranted.

and the challenges associated with navigating different service systems before finding veteran-specific opportunities. Service providers also expressed concerns that their outreach efforts were often thwarted by the inability to identify the veterans within their communities. Service providers also expressed concern that they had little connection with other organizations and resources that were similarly interested in serving veterans, making it difficult to create meaningful referral pathways. Veterans also expressed an interest in more opportunities to connect directly with other veterans, particularly to share experiences and offer help to their comrades.

There have been several attempts in other communities to facilitate better connections between the available services and veterans in need and among provider communities through collaborative networks or collective impact models that coordinate and synchronize service providers and enable an interface for veterans to learn about and access support.[2] If implemented within the metro Detroit area, these initiatives could serve to bridge the reported divide between service providers and veterans, as well as the disconnects with the service provider landscape and within the veteran community itself.

Enhancing Navigation Assistance

The current reliance upon word of mouth and personal connections with veteran service organizations and/or county-level veteran service officers is insufficient for ensuring all veterans in need understand the available benefits and resources. While the MVAA website (and the 1-800-MICH-VET line) provides important information about available federal- and state-level benefits for metro area veterans, other resources may be needed to help veterans understand what mental health resources may be available in their area. Right now, to find VA outpatient resources in the area, including mental health support, veterans can either contact the VA by phone or use the service locator on the VA website. To identify local community-based mental health

---

[2] See for example: Augusta Warrior Project (augustawarriorproject.org), NYC Serves (nycserves.org), Charlotte Bridge Home (www.charlottebridgehome.org), Illinois Joining Forces (www.illinoisjoiningforces.org), and the Los Angeles Veterans Collaborative (cir.usc.edu/community-engagement/la-vet-collaborative).

providers in the metro area, veterans can search the website directory listings of GaH, Star Behavioral Health Program, and the Substance Abuse Mental Health Administration's Behavioral Health Treatment Locator; they can also find providers through their employer-sponsored health plans. All of these approaches will likely produce lists of service providers, but the lists can still be uninformative, requiring the veteran to make several phone calls until they can identify an appropriate and available provider and schedule an appointment.

In other communities, organizations have implemented programs that provide one-stop navigation assistance. Some of these approaches utilize peers (e.g., buddytobuddy.org); and some utilize trained social workers to assess needs and make referrals. In these types of programs, veterans typically reach out to access a call center or a website, indicate the issue of concern or need, and are either provided with a warm hand-off to a trusted/vetted provider or given the information on available resources. Other programs utilize technology to enable this navigation assistance through an integrated website whereby veterans indicate their areas of need and customized, local lists of providers are generated (e.g., uniteus.com). Currently, multiple websites provide information about available resources in Michigan, which can be confusing. More work is needed to either create a consolidated web-based interface that links to all of the different sources or enhance/link existing navigation assistance approaches in the community.

Integrating Service Providers

Many of the stakeholder representatives from existing service organizations we spoke to were not aware of other service providers in the region. Thus, they were not able to make referrals to each other, nor were they able to understand how they could create partnerships to increase the efficiency in their own outreach efforts. At the same time, only a few of the organizations were routinely assessing the impact of their services. While the VCAT model in place within Region 10 is designed to help connect service providers to each other, several groups we spoke with reported that the current model of quarterly meetings was insufficient for creating meaningful connections and bridges for the veterans they serve, nor did it help them understand which organizations provided effective services for veterans. Other communities throughout the United States have adopted integration models to help create a stronger safety net and a "no wrong door" approach for veterans in need. Models vary, but efforts include Augusta Wounded Warrior (augustawarrior-project.org), AmericaServes (which is in North Carolina [ncserves.org] and New York City [nycserves.org]), and the Community BluePrint (pointsoflight.org/programs/military-initiatives/community-blueprint). Central to each of these initiatives is not only a capability to link services providers "on the backside" through technology and regular interactions, but also a capability to link the veteran directly to potential sources of support on a "front end," either through technology (such as UniteUs.com) or through human navigators and care facilitators. As organizations begin to increase collaboration or work toward integration, they will also need to work to demonstrate the impact of their efforts through more rigorous evaluations.

Connecting Veterans to Other Veterans

In our focus groups, veterans consistently reported their appreciation for being able to connect with other veterans, to share stories and information. They note a sense of connection and familiarity, which contributes to an ease in relationship building. These connections may also promote an opportunity to learn about how other veterans have navigated difficult issues and overcome mental health challenges. The American Legion and the VFW have several posts and halls throughout the region, and they historically have provided venues for these types of gatherings. However, concern was raised about whether newer generations of veterans were likely to gravitate to these types of settings. The use of social media (Facebook groups) was mentioned as a way to have veterans connect with each other, but it still requires the veterans to know about the groups and join them. The GPWM was featured earlier as one community-based organization that is working to enhance veteran connection opportunities in the community and provide a meeting/convening opportunity for veterans of all generations. In addition, Piquette Square is working to create its peer-to-peer drop-in program, and the Buddy-to-Buddy program already exists to link National Guard members to buddies for peer support and navigation assistance. However, many veterans in our focus groups noted continued interest in opportunities for face-to-face group meetings for information-sharing and socialization.

Filling Gaps in Resources

Many of the stakeholders and service providers with whom we spoke noted that they often had to restrict provision of services for veterans in their communities due to limited resources or capacity. Several specific limitations were noted by stakeholders: eligibility restrictions on benefits and services, limitations placed on the use of state-provided block grants to community mental health agencies, and limited capacity at vet centers to accommodate those interested in counseling services.

Examining and Expanding Eligibility Criteria

Many members of the Guard and Reserve community, as well as former service members who received a less than honorable discharge, are not able to access and utilize some of the benefits and services available to address veteran mental health problems. This group is often left to navigate the broader health and social support space, where they may face higher costs for care. Organizations and service providers that make mental health services available without regard to discharge or military service status can be an important resource for that community. There are some federally proposed efforts to re-examine discharge status for those veterans who may have experienced service-connected mental health problems, but if decisions are not overturned, many with "bad paper" or who lack deployment-related eligibility requirements will have limited access to the services available in the metro Detroit region.

Providing Funding Support to CMHAs

State-funded community mental health centers provide an important safety net for the most seriously ill residents, including veterans. However, budget limitations and criteria used to determine eligibility may often limit centers' abilities to meet the needs of veterans with mental health problems. Within the metro Detroit area, the community mental health centers reported an interest and willingness to serve veterans (some have also invested in specific military cultural competency training for their providers); however, they also noted that once a veteran is identified, he or she may wind up on a waiting list or being referred to the VA services. While VA-eligible veterans may be able to travel to the VA source of care or use their VA benefits to get treatment in the community (through one of the VA purchased-care programs), those veterans not eligible for VA care (including members of the National Guard or those who separated with less than honorable discharges), may be left without access to these important community mental health resources. As such, providing additional resources and creating specific priorities for address- ing veterans' needs in these settings may provide an additional safety net for veterans with mental health problems.

Expanding Vet Center Capacity

Several veterans and stakeholders reported a great affinity for the vet centers and their provision of nonmedical counseling and support to veterans and their spouses. However, several of the stakeholders also noted that the vet centers often had limited staffing capacity and had to rely heavily upon group-based approaches as a result. Given the popularity of vet centers, expanding their regional capacity through public-private partnerships with nongovernmental organizations could serve to open up access to additional support options for veterans with mental health problems.

Conclusion

The veterans residing in the metro Detroit area face challenges similar to veterans living in other areas. However, understanding the specific characteristics of and issues facing veterans in the Detroit community is important for ensuring that sufficient resources are available to meet potential demand within the local community. This study was spe- cifically focused on understanding the nature of mental health issues facing veterans in the metro Detroit region. From talking to veterans and stakeholders, we found concerns around PTSD, depression, and SUDs. These mental health issues may be related to earlier military experience (combat, deployment, injury) or associated with other chal- lenges they faced over time (relationship problems, unemployment, housing instability). While it was beyond our scope to quantify the exact magnitude of these issues among the veterans in the region, the stakeholders with whom we spoke repeatedly noted that there were many resources available to meet needs in the community but there were challenges in connecting veterans to them. For example, they noted that these resources could be hard to find and navigate; particularly for those who might be most vulnerable to these challenges, such as those with severe mental health problems, those living in poverty, and the homeless. Future efforts should focus on examining whether existing resources for these populations are working to identify veteran affiliation and to provide the appropriate high-quality mental health supports.

We also noted concerns among stakeholders about the early identification and treatment of mental health issues among veterans as a means of ensuring overall well-being and concerns about the availability and accessibility of VA mental health resources (e.g., appointment availability and transportation concerns), suggesting that additional programmatic efforts may be needed to connect veterans to the available services and resources within the region.

Recently, Detroit was named one of the 50 communities under the VA's new Veteran Economic Communities Initiative (VECI). This initiative has the opportunity to bring together local and national partners to coordinate services for veterans and their families (U.S. Department of Veterans Affairs, Office of Public Affairs, 2015). While primarily focused on economic empowerment and employment opportunities, this initiative could serve as the basis for expanding awareness of available services and programs for those with mental health problems. As the VECI brings local leaders together to form partnerships, improve policies, and create resource hubs that will help increase economic opportunities for veterans and their families, this may represent an opportunity for organizations that deliver mental health services and support to build even greater connections to ensure that veterans' mental health needs are met as well.

Illustrative Directory of Service Providers and Support Organizations in the Metro Detroit Area

This is not a comprehensive list of the services and support organizations that exist in the metro Detroit area. This is meant to be illustrative of the wide variety of existing organizations and services that are available to veterans and community members.

The organization's name and county or counties of operation (in some cases the headquarter location is listed) are listed in Table A.1, along with "Type" and whether they offer veteran-specific services or programs to veterans in the metro Detroit area. Type is labeled as "Service Provider" for organizations that provide either only mental health–related services or mental health services as one of the services they offer. "Support" indicates non-mental health–related services, such as housing and employment assistance. The "Veteran-Specific" column indicates whether an organization serves only the veteran population (Yes), has a program/service that is veteran-specific (Yes), or serves the general community (No).

Table A.1
Some Service Providers in Metro Detroit Area

Organization	County	Type	Veteran-Specific
Adult Well-Being Services	WAYNE	Service provider	No
Altarum Institute (Headquarters)	WASHTENAW	Network	Yes
American Association of Pastoral Counselors and Midwest Region	REGIONAL	Service provider	No
American Legion	WAYNE	Support	Yes
Americorps	INGHAM	Network	Yes
AMVETS	WAYNE	Support	Yes
Arab-American Chaldean Council	WAYNE	Service provider	No
Arab-American Community Center for Economic Social Service	WAYNE	Service provider	Yes
Army Community Services	MACOMB	Military	Yes
Behavioral Health Professionals, Inc.	WAYNE	Service provider	No
Blue Star Mothers	INGHAM	Support	Yes
Brain Injury Association of Michigan	LIVINGSTON	Service provider	Yes
Buddy-to-Buddy Volunteer Veteran Program	WASHTENAW	Support	Yes
Capuchin Soup Kitchen—Conner	WAYNE	Support	No
Capuchin Soup Kitchen—Meldrum	WAYNE	Support	No
CARE of Southeast Michigan	MACOMB	Service provider	No
Cass Community Social Services, Inc.	WAYNE	Support	No
ChristNet Daytime Program	WAYNE	Support	No
Coalition on Temporary Shelter	WAYNE	Support	No
Community Care Services	WAYNE	Service provider	No
Covenant House Michigan	WAYNE	Support	No
Dearborn Vet Center	WAYNE	Service provider	Yes
Detroit Central City	WAYNE	CMHA	No
Detroit Chamber of Commerce	WAYNE	Support	Yes
Detroit East, Inc.	WAYNE	CMHA	No
Detroit Recovery Project	WAYNE	Service provider	No
Detroit Rescue Mission Ministries—211 Glendale	WAYNE	Support	No
Detroit Rescue Mission Ministries—The Oasis	WAYNE	Support	No
Detroit Vet Center	WAYNE	Service provider	Yes
Detroit Wayne Mental Health Authority	WAYNE	CMHA	No
Developmental Centers, Inc.	WAYNE	Service provider	No

Table A.1—Continued

Organization	County	Type	Veteran-Specific
Disability Network/Wayne County and Detroit	WAYNE	Support	No
Disabled American Veterans	TRI-COUNTY	Support	Yes
East Eden Transitional Home	WAYNE	Support	No
Easter Seals	TRI-COUNTY	Service provider	Yes
Eastside Emergency Center	WAYNE	Support	No
Eastwood Clinics (St. John Providence)	MACOMB	Service provider	No
Effective Alternative for Community Housing	WAYNE	Support	No
Elmhurst Home	WAYNE	Service provider	No
Employer Support of the Guard and Reserve (ESGR)	INGHAM	Support	Yes
Equine Assisted Growth and Learning Association	ST. CLAIR	Service provider	Yes
Fallen & Wounded Soldier Fund	OAKLAND	Service provider	Yes
Family Assistance Center	WAYNE	Military	Yes
Give an Hour	TRI-COUNTY	Service provider	Yes
Goodwill Industries	WAYNE	Service provider	Yes
Grace Centers of Hope	OAKLAND	Support	No
Grosse Point War Memorial	WAYNE	Support	Yes
Guidance Center	WAYNE	Service provider	No
Hegira Programs	WAYNE	Service provider	No
Henry Ford Kingswood Hospital	OAKLAND	Hospital	No
Henry Ford Wyandotte Hospital	WAYNE	Hospital	No
HomeFront Strong Program	WASHTENAW	Support	Yes
HOPE Hospitality & Warming Center	OAKLAND	Support	No
Institute for Population Health	WAYNE	Support	No
Jefferson House	WAYNE	Support	No
John D. Dingell VA Medical Center	WAYNE	Hospital	Yes
Judah Transitional & Recovery House	WAYNE	Support	No
Lakeridge Village	WAYNE	Support	No
Lincoln Behavioral Services—Assertive Community Treatment	WASHTENAW	Service provider	No
M-SPAN Programs	WASHTENAW	Support	Yes
Macomb County Community Mental Health Services	MACOMB	CMHA	Yes
Macomb County Vet Center	MACOMB	Service provider	Yes
Macomb County Veterans Affairs	MACOMB	Support	Yes

Table A.1—Continued

Organization	County	Type	Veteran-Specific
Marine Corps League	TRI-COUNTY	Network	Yes
Mariners Inn	WAYNE	Service provider	No
Mental Health Association in Michigan	OAKLAND	Advocacy	No
Michigan Mental Health Counselors Association	Michigan	Network	No
Michigan Military Moms	TRI-COUNTY	Support	Yes
Michigan National Guard Family Programs	INGHAM	Military	Yes
Michigan Psychiatric Society	Michigan	Advocacy	No
Michigan Psychological Association	Michigan	Advocacy	No
Michigan Talent Connect	TRI-COUNTY	Support	Yes
Michigan Veterans Affairs Agency	INGHAM	Support	Yes
Michigan Veterans Foundation	WAYNE	Service provider	Yes
Michigan Veterans Task Force	TRI-COUNTY	Support	Yes
Michigan Wounded Warrior Project	REGIONAL	Service provider	Yes
Military Order of the Purple Heart	WAYNE	Support	Yes
Military Spouses of Michigan	WASHTENAW	Support	Yes
Motor City Blight Busters—Veteran's Village Center	WAYNE	Support	Yes
National Alliance on Mental Illness and Michigan Chapter	INGHAM	Support	No
Neighborhood Service Organization—Tumaini Center	WAYNE	Service provider	No
New Center Community Services	WAYNE	Service provider	No
North Central Health Center	WAYNE	Service provider	No
Northeast Guidance Center	WAYNE	Service provider	No
Oakland Community College	OAKLAND	Support	Yes
Oakland County Community Mental Health Authority	OAKLAND	CMHA	Yes
Oakland County Veterans Affairs	OAKLAND	Support	Yes
Oakland University	OAKLAND	Support	Yes
Open Door Rescue Mission Ministries	WAYNE	Support	No
Operation Get Down	WAYNE	Service provider	No
Operation Homefront	EATON	Service provider	Yes
Paralyzed Veterans of America	OAKLAND	Support	Yes
Philip House Mission	WAYNE	Support	No
Pontiac Community Based Outpatient Clinic	OAKLAND	Service provider	Yes
Pontiac Vet Center	OAKLAND	Service provider	Yes

Table A.1—Continued

Organization	County	Type	Veteran-Specific
Quality Behavioral Health, Inc.	WAYNE	Service provider	No
Red Cross	TRI-COUNTY	Service provider	Yes
Safe Haven Detroit	WAYNE	Support	No
Salvation Army	TRI-COUNTY	Support	Yes
Salvation Army MATTS	MACOMB	Support	No
Selfridge Air National Guard Base-Family Services	MACOMB	Military	Yes
Sinai Grace Hospital—Crisis Center	WAYNE	Hospital	No
Skyline Outreach Ministries	WAYNE	Support	No
South Oakland Shelter (SOS)	OAKLAND	Support	No
Southeast Michigan Stand Down	WAYNE	Support	Yes
Southfield Veterans Commission	OAKLAND	Support	Yes
Southwest Counseling Solutions	WAYNE	Service Provider	Yes
St. Mary Mercy Hospital of Livonia	WAYNE	Hospital	No
STAR Behavioral Health Providers	TRI-COUNTY	Network	Yes
Starfish Family Services	WAYNE	Support	No
Starfish Family Services Crisis Shelter	WAYNE	Service provider	No
Stiggy's Dogs	LIVINGSTON	Service provider	Yes
Stone Crest Behavioral Health Center	WAYNE	Service provider	No
STRoNG Military Families Program	WASHTENAW	Support	Yes
Student Veterans of America	TRI-COUNTY	Support	Yes
Suits for Soldiers	OAKLAND	Support	Yes
Team Mental Health—Eastern Market Clinic	WAYNE	Service provider	No
Team Mental Health—Southgate Clinic	WAYNE	Service provider	No
Team Red, White & Blue	WASHTENAW	Support	Yes
United States Army Reserve Family Support Center	OAKLAND	Military	Yes
United Way	WAYNE	Support	Yes
University Physicians Group—Psychiatric Center	WAYNE	Service provider	No
Veteran's Refuge Network	WASHTENAW	Service provider	Yes
Veterans Community Action Team	TRI-COUNTY	Network	Yes
Veterans of Foreign Wars	TRI-COUNTY	Support	Yes
Vets Returning Home	MACOMB	Support	Yes
Vietnam Veterans of America	WAYNE	Network	Yes

Table A.1—Continued

Organization	County	Type	Veteran-Specific
Volunteers of America	TRI-COUNTY	Support	Yes
Wayne County Family Center	WAYNE	Support	No
Wayne County Mental Health Authority	WAYNE	CMHA	No
Wayne County Veterans Affairs	WAYNE	Support	Yes
Wayne State University	WAYNE	Support	Yes
Wayne State University Physician Group – Psychiatry	WAYNE	Service provider	No
Welcome Inn Day Center for the Homeless	OAKLAND	Support	No
Wins for Warriors Foundation	WAYNE	Support	Yes

Abbreviations

CBT	cognitive behavioral therapy
CMH	community mental health
CMHA	County Mental Health Authority
DWMHA	Detroit Wayne Mental Health Authority
EMDR	eye movement desensitization and reprocessing
GaH	Give an Hour
GPWM	Grosse Pointe War Memorial
MCPN	managers of comprehensive provider networks
MIVCAT	Michigan Veterans Community Action Teams
MOS	military occupational specialty
MVAA	Michigan Veterans Affairs Agency
MVTF	Michigan Veteran Trust Fund
NAMI	National Alliance for the Mentally Ill
PTSD	posttraumatic stress disorder
SBHP	STAR Behavioral Health Provider
SSVF	Supportive Services for Veteran Families
SUD	substance use disorders
TBI	traumatic brain injury
VA	Department of Veterans Affairs
VCAT	Veteran Community Action Team
VECI	Veteran Economic Communities Initiative

VFW	Veterans of Foreign Wars
VISN	Veteran Integrated Service Network
VOA	Volunteers of America

References

Altarum Institute, *Michigan Veterans Community Action Teams: Detroit Metro Veteran Focus Groups Report*, Ann Arbor, Mich.: September 10, 2014. As of September 23, 2015:
http://altarum.org/sites/default/files/uploaded-publication-files/Altarum%20 Detroit%20Metro%20Focus%20Group%20Report%20Final%20Delivered%20 20140910.pdf

American Academy of Nursing, *Have You Ever Served in the Military?* undated. As of November 16, 2015:
http://www.haveyoueverserved.com

American Foundation for Suicide Prevention, *Facts and Figures*, 2013. As of November 17, 2015:
https://www.afsp.org/understanding-suicide/facts-and-figures

Austin, D., "How Metro Detroit Transit Went from Best to Worst," *Detroit Free Press*, February 2015. As of October 20, 2015:
http://www.freep.com/story/news/local/2015/02/06/ michigan-detroit-public-transit/22926133/

Backer, T., and E. Howard, "Cognitive Impairments and the Prevention of Homelessness: Research and Practice Review," *Journal of Primary Prevention*, Vol. 28, Nos. 3–4, 2007, pp. 375–388.

Bankier, B., and A. B. Littman, "Psychiatric Disorders and Coronary Heart Disease in Women—A Still Neglected Topic: Review of the Literature from 1971 to 2000," *Psychotherapy and Psychosomatics*, Vol. 71, No. 3, 2002, pp. 133–140.

Bashford, J., C. Collins, S. Hasan, and Lord Patel of Bradford, *Call to Mind: A Framework for Action, Findings from the Review of Veterans and Family Members Mental and Related Health Needs Assessments*, Community Innovations Enterprise, 2015. As of October 14, 2015:
http://www.fim-trust.org/wp-content/uploads/2015/07/20150623-Call-to-MInd-Executive-Summary-23rd-June-20151.pdf

Beardslee, W. R., J. Bemporad, M. B. Keller, and G. L. Klerman, "Children of Parents with Major Affective Disorder: A Review," *American Journal of Psychiatry*, Vol. 140, No. 7, 1983, pp. 825–832.

Beardslee, W. R., E. M. Versage, and T. R. Gladstone, "Children of Affectively Ill Parents: A Review of the Past 10 Years," *Journal of the American Academy of Child and Adolescent Psychiatry*, Vol. 37, 1998, pp. 1134–1141.

Boscarino, J. A. "External-Cause Mortality After Psychologic Trauma: The Effects of Stress Exposure and Predisposition," *Comprehensive Psychiatry*, Vol. 47, No. 6, 2006a, pp. 503–514.

———, "Posttraumatic Stress Disorder and Mortality Among U.S. Army Veterans 30 Years After Military Service," *Annals of Epidemiology*, Vol. 16, No. 4, 2006b, p. 9.

Boscarino, J. A., and J. Chang, "Electrocardiogram Abnormalities Among Men with Stress-Related Psychiatric Disorders: Implications for Coronary Heart Disease and Clinical Research," *Annals of Behavioral Medicine*, Vol. 21, No. 3, 1999, pp. 227–234.

Brown, R. A., G. N. Marshall, J. Breslau, C. Farris, K. Chan Osilla, H. A. Pincus, T. Ruder, P. Voorhies, D. Barnes-Proby, K. Pfrommer, L. Miyashiro, Y. Rana, and D. M. Adamson, *Access to Behavioral Health Care for Geographically Remote Service Members and Dependents in the U.S.*, Santa Monica, Calif.: RAND Corporation, RR-578-OSD, 2015. As of August 17, 2015:
http://www.rand.org/pubs/research_reports/RR578

Burke, M. N., "Thousands of Michigan Veterans Miss Out on Benefits," *Detroit News*, April 1, 2015. As of November 16, 2015:
http://www.detroitnews.com/story/news/politics/2015/03/31/
thousands-michigan-veterans-miss-benefits/70752468/

Burnam, M. A., et al., "Systems of Care: Challenges and Opportunities to Improve Access to High-Quality Care," in T. Tanielian and L. H. Jaycox, eds., *Invisible Wounds of War: Psychological and Cognitive Injuries, Their Consequences and Services to Assist Recovery*, Santa Monica, Calif.: RAND Corporation, MG-720-CCF, April 2008, pp. 245–428. As of November 16, 2015:
http://www.rand.org/pubs/monographs/MG720.html

Burnam, M. A., and K. E. Watkins, "Substance Abuse with Mental Disorders: Specialized Public Systems and Integrated Care," *Health Affairs*, Vol. 25, No. 3, 2006, pp. 648–658.

Callender, C. O., and P. V. Miles, "Minority Organ Donation: The Power of an Educated Community," *Journal of the American College of Surgeons*, Vol. 210, No. 5, 2010, pp. 708–715.

Carroll, E. M., D. B. Rueger, D. W. Foy, and C. P. Donahoe, "Vietnam Combat Veterans with Posttraumatic Stress Disorder: Analysis of Marital and Cohabitating Adjustment," *Journal of Abnormal Psychology*, Vol. 94, No. 3, 1985, pp. 329–337.

Carter, P., "The Vets We Reject and Ignore," *New York Times*, November 11, 2013.

Carter, P., and K. Kidder, *Needs Assessment: Veterans in the Western United States*, Center for a New American Security, 2013. As of 14 October 2015: http://www.cnas.org/sites/default/files/publications-pdf/CNAS_NeedsAssessment_CarterKidder.pdf

Castro, C. A., S. Kintzle, and A. Hassan, *The State of the American Veteran: The Orange County Veterans Study*, Los Angeles Calif.: USC School of Social Work, Center for Innovation and Research on Veterans & Military Families, February 2015. As of October 14, 2015: http://cir.usc.edu/wp-content/uploads/2015/02/OC-Veterans-Study_USC-CIR_Feb-2015.pdf

Center for Mental Health Services, *Co-Occurring Disorders: Integrated Dual Disorders Treatment Implementation Resource Kit (Draft Version)*, 2003. As of February 15, 2006: http://www.wvbhpc.org/docs/IDDTinfoPMHAAJ1_04.pdf

Cummings, E. M., and P. T. Davies, "Depressed Parents and Family Functioning: Interpersonal Effects and Children's Functioning and Development," in T. E. Joiner and J. C. Coyne, eds., *The Interactional Nature of Depression: Advances in Interpersonal Approaches*, Washington, D.C: American Psychological Association, 1999, pp. 299–327.

Davidson, J. R., R. D. Smith, and H. S. Kudler, "Familial Psychiatric Illness in Chronic Posttraumatic Stress Disorder," *Comprehensive Psychiatry*, Vol. 30, No. 4, 1989, pp. 339–345.

Demyttenare, K., R. Bruffaerts, S. Lee, et al., Mental Disorders Among Persons with Chronic Back or Neck Pain: Results from the World Mental Health Surveys," *Pain*, Vol. 129, No. 3, June 2007, pp. 332–342.

Desai M. U., A. J. Pavlo, L. Davidson, I. Harpaz-Rotem, and R. A. Rosenheck, "'I Want to Come Home,' Vietnam-Era Veterans Presenting for Mental Health Care, Roughly 40 Years After Vietnam," *Psychiatric Quarterly*, July 9, 2015.

Ettner, S. L., R. G. Frank, and R. C. Kessler, "The Impact of Psychiatric Disorders on Labor Market Outcomes," *Industrial and Labor Relations Review*, Vol. 51, No. 1, 1997, pp. 64–81.

Gonzalez, E. A., J. N. Dieter, R. A. Natale, and S. L. Tanner, "Neuropsychological Evaluation of Higher Functioning Homeless Persons: A Comparison of an Abbreviated Test Battery to the Mini-Mental State Exam," *Journal of Nervous and Mental Disease*, Vol. 189, No. 3, 2001, pp. 176–181.

Greenberg, P. E., R. C. Kessler, H. G. Birnbaum, S. A. Leong, et al., "The Economic Burden of Depression in the United States: How Did It Change Between 1990 and 2000?" *Journal of Clinical Psychiatry*, Vol. 64, No. 12, 2003, pp. 1465–1475.

Hasin, D. S., R. D. Goodwin, F. S. Stinson, and B. F. Grant, "Epidemiology of Major Depressive Disorder: Results from the National Epidemiologic Survey on Alcoholism and Related Conditions," *Archives of General Psychiatry*, Vol. 62, No. 10, 2005, pp. 1097–1106.

Hermes, E. D., R. Hoff, R. A. Rosenheck, "Sources of Increasing Number of Vietnam-Era Veterans with a Diagnosis of PTSD Using VHA Services," *Psychiatric Services*, Vol. 65, No. 6, June 1, 2014, pp. 830–832.

Hoffmire, C. A., J. E. Kemp, and R. M. Bossarte, "Changes in Suicide Mortality for Veterans and Non Veterans by Gender and History of VHA Service Use, 2000–2010," *Psychiatric Services*, Vol. 66, No. 9, September 1, 2015, pp. 959–965.

Hoge, C. W., A. Terhakopian, C. A. Castro, S. C. Messer, and C. C. Engel, "Association of Posttraumatic Stress Disorder with Somatic Symptoms, Health Care Visits, and Absenteeism Among Iraq War Veterans," *American Journal of Psychiatry*, Vol. 164, No. 1, 2007, pp. 150–153.

Jordan, B. K., C. R. Marmar, J. A. Fairbank, W. E. Schlenger, R. A. Kulka, R. L. Hough, et al., "Problems in Families of Male Vietnam Veterans with Posttraumatic Stress Disorder," *Journal of Consulting and Clinical Psychology*, Vol. 60, No. 6, 1992, pp. 916–926.

Karney, B. R., et al., "Predicting the Immediate and Long-Term Consequences of Post-Traumatic Stress Disorder, Depression, and Traumatic Brain Injury in Veterans of Operation Enduring Freedom and Operation Iraqi Freedom 2008," in T. Tanielian and L. H. Jaycox, eds., *Invisible Wounds of War: Psychological and Cognitive Injuries, Their Consequences and Services to Assist Recovery*, Santa Monica, Calif.: RAND Corporation, MG-720-CCF, April 2008, pp. 119–166. As of November 16, 2015:
http://www.rand.org/pubs/monographs/MG720.html

Kavanagh D. J., et al., "Contrasting Views and Experiences of Health Professionals on the Management of Comorbid Substance Misuse and Mental Disorders," *Australian and New Zealand Journal of Psychiatry*, Vol. 34, No. 2, 2000, pp. 279–289.

Kessler, R. C., G. Borges, and E. E. Walters, "Prevalence of and Risk Factors for Lifetime Suicide Attempts in the National Comorbidity Survey," *Archives of General Psychiatry*, Vol. 56, No. 7, 1999, pp. 617–626.

Kessler, R. C., W. T. Chiu, O. Demler, and E. E. Walters, "Prevalence, Severity, and Comorbidity of 12-Month DSM-IV Disorders in the National Comorbidity Survey Replication," *Archives of General Psychiatry*, Vol. 62, No. 6, 2005, pp. 617–627.

Kessler, R. C., C. B. Nelson, K. A. McGonagle, M. J. Edlund, R. G. Frank, and P. J. Leaf, "The Epidemiology of Co-Occurring Addictive and Mental Disorders: Implications for Prevention and Service Utilization," *American Journal of Orthopsychiatry*, Vol. 66, No. 1, 1996, pp. 17–31.

Kessler, R. C., A. Sonnega, E. Bromet, M. Hughes, et al., "Posttraumatic Stress Disorder in the National Comorbidity Survey," *Archives of General Psychiatry*, Vol. 52, No. 12, 1995, pp. 1048–1060.

Kessler, R. C., E. E. Walters, and M. S. Forthofer, "The Social Consequences of Psychiatric Disorders, III: Probability of Marital Stability," *American Journal of Psychiatry*, Vol. 155, No. 8, 1998, pp. 1092–1096.

Kulka, R. A., W. E. Schlenger, J. A. Fairbank, R. L. Hough, et al., *Trauma and the Vietnam War Generation: Report of Findings from the National Vietnam Veterans Readjustment Study*, Philadelphia, Pa.: Brunner/Mazel, 1990.

Livingston, J. D., A. Tugwell, K. Korf-Uzan, M. Cianfrone, and C. Coniglio, "Evaluation of a Campaign to Improve Awareness and Attitudes of Young People Towards Mental Health Issues," *Social Psychiatry and Psychiatric Epidemiology*, Vol. 48, No. 6, 2013, pp. 965–973.

MacDonald, C., K. Chamberlain, N. Long, and R. Flett, "Posttraumatic Stress Disorder and Interpersonal Functioning in Vietnam War Veterans: A Mediational Model," *Journal of Traumatic Stress*, Vol. 12, No. 4, 1999, pp. 701–707.

Magruder, K. M., B. C. Frueh, R. G. Knapp, M. R. Johnson, et al., "PTSD Symptoms, Demographic Characteristics, and Functional Status Among Veterans Treated in VA Primary Care Clinics," *Journal of Trauma and Stress*, Vol. 17, No. 4, 2004, pp. 293–301.

Mann, J. J., A. Apter, J. Bertolote, A. Beautrais, et al., "Suicide Prevention Strategies: A Systematic Review," *Journal of the American Medical Association*, Vol. 294, No. 16, 2005, pp. 2064–2074.

McCarren, M., G. R. Janes, J. Goldberg, S. A. Eisen, W. R. True, and W. G. Henderson, "A Twin Study of the Association of Post-Traumatic Stress Disorder and Combat Exposure with Long-Term Socioeconomic Status in Vietnam Veterans," *Journal of Trauma and Stress*, Vol. 8, No. 1, 1995, pp. 111–124.

Mueser, K. T., ed., *Integrated Treatment for Dual Disorders: A Guide to Effective Practice*, Guilford Press, 2003.

Myer, T., *Serving Those Who Served*, Philanthropy Roundtable Report, 2013. As of September 29, 2015:
http://www.philanthropyroundtable.org/file_uploads/Serving_Those_Who_Served.pdf

North, C. S., and E. M. Smith, "Posttraumatic Stress Disorder Among Homeless Men and Women." *Hospital and Community Psychiatry*, Vol. 43, No. 10, 1992, pp. 1010–1016.

Ramchand, R., J. Acosta, R. M. Burns, L. H. Jaycox, and C. G. Pernin, *The War Within: Preventing Suicide in the U.S. Military*, Santa Monica, Calif.: RAND Corporation, MG-953-OSD, 2011. As of August 18, 2015:
http://www.rand.org/pubs/monographs/MG953

Ramchand R., R. Rudavsky, S. Grant, T. Tanielian, and L. Jaycox, "Prevalence of, Risk Factors for, and Consequences of Posttraumatic Stress Disorder and Other Mental Health Problems in Military Populations Deployed to Iraq and Afghanistan," *Current Psychiatry Report*, Vol. 17, No. 5, May 2015, pp. 1–11.

Ramchand R., T. L. Schell, L. H. Jaycox, and T. L. Tanielian, "Epidemiology of Trauma Events and Mental Health Outcomes Associated with War-Zone Deployment," in J. Ruzek, P. Schnurr, M. Friedman, and J. Vasterling, eds., *Veterans of the Global War on Terror*, American Psychological Association, 2010.

Ramchand R., T. Tanielian, M. P. Fisher, C. A. Vaughan, T. E. Trail, C. Epley, P. Voorhies, M. W. Robbins, E. Robinson, and B. Ghosh-Dastida, *Hidden Heroes: America's Military Caregivers*, Santa Monica, Calif.: RAND Corporation, RR-499-TEDF, April 2014. As of November 16, 2015:
http://www.rand.org/pubs/research_reports/RR499.html

Reger, B., L. Cooper, S. Booth-Butterfield, H. Smith, A. Bauman, M. Wootan, S. Middlestadt, B. Marcus, and F. Greer, "Wheeling Walks: A Community Campaign Using Paid Media to Encourage Walking Among Sedentary Older Adults," *Preventive Medicine*, Vol. 35, No. 3, 2002, pp. 285–292.

Regier, D. A., M. E. Farmer, D. S. Rae, B. Z. Locke, et al., "Comorbidity of Mental Disorders with Alcohol and Other Drug Abuse: Results from the Epidemiologic Catchment Area (ECA) Study," *Journal of the American Medical Association*, Vol. 264, No. 19, 1990, pp. 2511–2518.

Riggs, D. S., C. A. Byrne, F. W. Weathers, and B. T. Litz, "The Quality of the Intimate Relationships of Male Vietnam Veterans: Problems Associated with Posttraumatic Stress Disorder," *Journal of Traumatic Stress*, Vol. 11, No. 1, 1998, pp. 87–101.

Rosenheck, R., C. Leda, L. K. Frishman, J. Lam, and A.-M. Chung, "Homeless Veterans," in J. Baumohl, ed., *Homelessness in America: A Reference Book*, Phoenix, Ariz.: Oryx Press, 1996, pp. 97–108.

Roth, D., "Homeless Veterans: Comparisons with Other Homeless Men," in M. J. Robertson and M. Greenblatt, eds., *Homelessness: A National Perspective*, New York, N.Y.: Plenum Press, 1992.

Rugulies, R., "Depression as a Predictor for Coronary Heart Disease: A Review and Meta-Analysis," *American Journal of Preventive Medicine*, Vol. 23, No. 1, 2002, pp. 51–61.

Savoca, E., and R. Rosenheck, "The Civilian Labor Market Experiences of Vietnam-Era Veterans: The Influence of Psychiatric Disorders," *Journal of Mental Health Policy and Economics*, Vol. 3, No. 4, 2000, pp. 199–207.

Schell, Terry L., Terri Tanielian, Carrie M. Farmer, Lisa H. Jaycox, Grant N. Marshall, Terry L. Schell, Terri Tanielian, Christine Anne Vaughan and Glenda Wrenn, *A Needs Assessment of New York State Veterans: Final Report to the New York State Health Foundation*, Santa Monica, Calif.: RAND Corporation, TR-920-NYSHF, 2011. As of August 18, 2015:
http://www.rand.org/pubs/technical_reports/TR920

Schnurr, P. P., and B. L. Green, *Trauma and Health: Physical Health Consequences of Exposure to Extreme Stress*, Washington, D.C.: American Psychological Association Press, 2004.

Schnurr, P. P., A. F. Hayes, C. A. Lunney, M. McFall, and M. Uddo, "Longitudinal Analysis of the Relationship Between Symptoms and Quality of Life in Veterans Treated for Posttraumatic Stress Disorder," *Journal of Consulting and Clinical Psychology*, Vol. 74, No. 4, 2006, pp. 707–713.

Sharp, M. L., N. T. Fear, R. J. Rona, et al., "Stigma as a Barrier to Seeking Health Care Among Military Personnel with Mental Health Problems," *Epidemiologic Reviews*, Vol. 37, No. 1, 2015, pp. 144–162.

Smith, M. W., P. P. Schnurr, and R. A. Rosenheck, "Employment Outcomes and PTSD Symptom Severity," *Mental Health Services Research*, Vol. 7, No. 2, 2005, pp. 89–101.

Smolenski, D. J., M. A. Reger, C. L. Alexander, N. A. Skopp, N. E. Bush, D. D. Luxton, and G. A. Gahm, *DODSER: Department of Defense Suicide Event Report: Calendar Year 2012 Annual Report*, Washington, D.C.: Department of Defense, 2013.

Solter, V., V. Thaller, D. Karlović, and D. Crnković, "Elevated Serum Lipids in Veterans with Combat-Related Chronic Posttraumatic Stress Disorder," *Croatian Medical Journal*, Vol. 43, No. 6, 2002, pp. 685–689.

State of Michigan, *Executive Reorganization of Department of Military and Veterans Affairs: Creation of the Michigan Veterans Affairs Agency*, Executive Order No. 2013–2, January 18, 2013. As of November 30, 2015: https://www.michigan.gov/documents/snyder/EO_2013-2_408988_7.pdf

Sullivan, G., A. Burnam, P. Koegel, and J. Hollenberg, "Quality of Life of Homeless Persons with Mental Illness: Results from the Course-of-Homelessness Study," *Psychiatric Services*, Vol. 51, No. 9, 2000, pp. 1135–1141.

Susser, E. S., S. P. Lin, and S. A. Conover, "Risk Factors for Homelessness Among Patients Admitted to a State Mental Hospital," *American Journal of Psychiatry*, Vol. 148, No. 12, 1991, pp. 1659–1664.

Szymendera, S. D., *Who Is a "Veteran"?—Basic Eligibility for Veterans' Benefits*, Washington, D.C.: Congressional Research Service, R42324, 2015. https://www.fas.org/sgp/crs/misc/R42324.pdf

Tanielian, T., C. Farris, C. Batka, C. M. Farmer, E. Robinson, C. C. Engel, M. Robbins, and L. H. Jaycox, *Ready to Serve: Community-Based Provider Capacity to Deliver Culturally Competent, Quality Mental Health Care to Veterans and Their Families*, Santa Monica, Calif.: RAND Corporation, RR-806-UNHF, 2014. As of November 13, 2015: http://www.rand.org/pubs/research_reports/RR806.html

Tanielian, T., and L. H. Jaycox, eds., *Invisible Wounds of War: Psychological and Cognitive Injuries, Their Consequences and Services to Assist Recovery*, Santa Monica, Calif.: RAND Corporation, MG-720-CCF, 2008. As of November 13, 2015:
http://www.rand.org/pubs/monographs/MG720.html

U.S. Code, Title 38, Veterans' Benefits, Section 101, Definitions. As of November 30, 2015:
https://www.law.cornell.edu/uscode/text/38/101

U.S. Department of Veterans Affairs, National Center for Veterans Analysis and Statistics, *Expenditures*, updated October 9, 2015. As of November 16, 2015:
http://www.va.gov/vetdata/Expenditures.asp

U.S. Department of Veterans Affairs, Office of the Actuary, *Veteran Population Projection, Model 2014*, updated September 2015. As of October 2015:
http://www.va.gov/vetdata/Veteran_Population.asp

U.S. Department of Veterans Affairs, Office of Public Affairs, *State Summary: Michigan*, undated. As of November 16, 2015:
http://www.va.gov/vetdata/docs/SpecialReports/State_Summaries_Michigan.pdf

———, "VA Announces Expansion of Veterans Economic Communities Initiative," September 30, 2015. As of November 17, 2015:
http://www.va.gov/opa/pressrel/pressrelease.cfm?id=2732

VA—*See* U.S. Department of Veterans Affairs.

Watkins, K. E., et al., "Review of Treatment Recommendations for Persons with a Co-Occurring Affective or Anxiety and Substance Use Disorder," *Psychiatric Services*, Vol. 56, No. 8, 2005, pp. 913–926.

Wells, K. B., A. Stewart, R. D. Hays, M. A. Burnam, W. Rogers, M. Daniels, et al. "The Functioning and Well-Being of Depressed Patients: Results from the Medical Outcomes Study," *Journal of the American Medical Association*, Vol. 262, No. 7, 1989, pp. 914–919.

Wulsin, L. R., G. E. Vaillant, and V. E. Wells, "A Systematic Review of the Mortality of Depression," *Psychosomatics Medicine*, Vol. 61, No. 1, 1999, pp. 6–17.

Zatzick, D. F., C. R. Marmar, D. S. Weiss, W. S. Browner, T. J. Metzler, J. M. Golding, et al., "Posttraumatic Stress Disorder and Functioning and Quality of Life Outcomes in a Nationally Representative Sample of Male Vietnam Veterans," *American Journal of Psychiatry*, Vol. 154, No. 12, 1997, pp. 1690–1695.

Zinzow, H. M., T. W. Britt, C. L. S. Pury, M. A. Raymond, A. C. McFadden, and C. M. Burnette, "Barriers and Facilitators of Mental Health Treatment Seeking Among Active-Duty Army Personnel," *Military Psychology*, Vol. 25, No. 5, 2013, pp. 514–535.

Zubin, J., and B. Spring, "Vulnerability—A New View of Schizophrenia," *Journal of Abnormal Psychology*, Vol. 86, 1977, pp. 103–126.